Praise

'A fabulous and informative book, packed with golden nuggets of information on all aspects of flipping properties.'
— **Dave Drimmie**, founder of The Profit Champions

'If you want to know anything about property staging for success, read this book and learn from one of the best.'
— **Daniel Priestley**, CEO, Dent Global

Flip AND Fly

The secret to sustainable
and profitable property renovation

Angela Drakeford

Re^ethink

First published in Great Britain in 2024
by Rethink Press (www.rethinkpress.com)

© Copyright Angela Drakeford

All rights reserved. No part of this publication may be reproduced, stored in or introduced into a retrieval system, or transmitted, in any form, or by any means (electronic, mechanical, photocopying, recording or otherwise) without the prior written permission of the publisher.

The right of Angela Drakeford to be identified as the author of this work has been asserted by her in accordance with the Copyright, Designs and Patents Act 1988.

This book is sold subject to the condition that it shall not, by way of trade or otherwise, be lent, resold, hired out, or otherwise circulated without the publisher's prior consent in any form of binding or cover other than that in which it is published and without a similar condition including this condition being imposed on the subsequent purchaser.

Cover image © Shutterstock | inimalGraphic and Isma Design

Contents

Foreword	1
Introduction	3
PART ONE Getting Ready	**9**
1 What Is House Flipping And Why Is It For You?	**11**
What is house flipping?	13
Flipping to sell or rent	16
That flippin' house: Understanding your 'why', mission and vision	18
Why this business isn't for softies	23
2 The Developer's Mindset	**25**
It's not about you: The business mindset	26
What do successful flippers do?	29
Making a business plan	35
Understand your tasks	41
Who can help you?	42
Summary	43

3	The Property Market	45
	Understanding the market	46
	Recessions and booms in the property market	48
	Understanding your ceiling price	49
	Building communities while property flipping	51
	Summary	53
4	Finding Your Investment Property	55
	Auctions	56
	Property portals	61
	Estate agents	64
	Non-platform ways of property hunting	65
	The right property for the right area	73
	How to recognise up-and-coming areas	76
	Who is your property for?	78
	Due diligence	79
	Evaluating the property	81
	Summary	83
5	Securing The Deal	85
	Understanding your finances: A checklist	87
	Raising the finances with zero funds	88
	Types of mortgages	92
	Buy-to-develop grants	95
	Understanding chains	96
	Tax implications (capital gains)	99

Stamp duty	100
The sales process	101
Belt and braces: What survey do you need?	104
The final hurdles: How to make time move faster	105
Summary	106

PART TWO Getting It Right — 109

6 Managing Your Project — 111

Who is on your team?	112
Planning permission and building regulations	116
The design process	120
Finding reputable tradespeople	125
Set yourself up for success	129
The tender process	132
Summary	137

7 Keys For Maximising Return On Investment — 141

Which rooms will give you the best ROI?	142
What else will yield the biggest ROI?	144
Material world: When to invest in quality	146
Usable outside space	150
Finishing touches	151
Kerb appeal: How first impressions last	152
Summary	154

8	**On Your Marks, Get Set, Stage**	**157**
	What is property staging?	159
	How staging works	160
	Why stage a property?	162
	Your five-step staging roadmap	164
	Summary	177

PART THREE Getting It Sold — **179**

9	**Selling The Lifestyle**	**181**
	Professional photography vs estate agents' services	182
	How to source a professional photographer	184
	DIY photography	190
	Professional vs DIY photos	191
	Summary	195
10	**Sealing The Deal**	**197**
	Estate agents vs DIY selling	198
	Offers and counter offers	200
	Summary	201
11	**Preparing To Fly**	**203**
	The five-, ten- and twenty-year plan	204
	The joy of outsourcing	205
	Effective delegation	205

Building professional relationships	207
Flying high to the next level	211
Summary	212
Conclusion	**215**
Acknowledgements	**221**
The author	**223**

All author royalties from this book will be donated to a fantastic charity close to my heart, MOBIE.

MOBIE is an educational charity, set up by TV presenter and architect George Clarke to inspire young people to build the homes of the future: As George explains, 'I started MOBIE to create a generational shift, to inspire you to deliver the homes we want and really need. Homes that are green, affordable, promote well-being and that are amazing spaces to live in.'

Their work involves educating young people on the importance of quality, sustainability and innovation within the design and construction industry. It sets up challenges all over the country for young people to get involved and showcase their ideas.

www.mobie.org.uk

For my grandad, who taught me from a young age that working hard and taking risks reaps rewards and allows you to fly high.

For my mum and dad, who have always been by my side through thick and thin. Without their influence and work ethic, this book wouldn't have been possible.

For my husband, Rob, and my boys, for always keeping me grounded when flying.

Foreword

Since becoming a Dent KPI alumni, Angela has fast become a key person of influence and the go-to person in the property staging industry.

Her thirty years of professional experience as an interior designer has set her apart from her peers, with the added benefit of her property staging and development associations.

Her wealth of knowledge is paramount throughout this book. She has clearly and articulately demonstrated how to avoid all the pitfalls of property flipping from the beginning of the journey right through to the end, giving the reader all the inside secrets of how to gain maximum return on investment in all aspects of the journey. Her knowledge is backed up by the years of experience of both her and the close associations she has made along the way.

This is *the* must-have book for anyone setting out on their property development journey.

— **Daniel Priestley**, CEO, Dent Global

Introduction

Three seconds… that's how long a property listed on Rightmove in today's competitive housing market has to connect with a potential buyer or tenant.

It's no wonder with so much competition that many small developers find themselves stuck in 'limbo land', unable to sell their properties with a good profit and sustainable approach in order to move on to the next and grow their dream business of becoming a successful property developer.

Being a professional interior designer and property stager, I meet many homeowners and small property developers who have spent time, effort and money on a property just to have it sitting on the market, draining their finances and energy, unable to sell it with a decent return on investment (ROI).

They can't understand why this is happening to them as the property down the road sold within a week of the sale board going up. Their property is in a great area and they have given their all to its renovation, so why won't it sell? They feel stuck in limbo, with their business and life on hold.

I understand that desperation. In 2015 when I returned to the UK as a newly single parent, I needed to sell my family home and my investment property quickly. I was desperate for capital to rebuild my life, but the properties didn't sell and the drain on my finances almost triggered a breakdown.

I'd had a global career in interior design for over two decades at that point – half of it running my own business – and in 2017 I had the opportunity to work for a huge property developer in Manchester. This was where I gained my first insider knowledge of all aspects of property development: acquisition, procurement, budget, planning, good sustainability practices and construction. I worked closely with the owner, a forward-thinking and energetic property developer, and helped him turn his vision into reality, having insights on the marketing collateral and how the decisions made at this stage vastly influenced the target market and ROI on his properties.

INTRODUCTION

I also worked alongside the lettings and sales team, styling the apartments for rental and sale. It was here that my passion for property staging grew. I had the idea of staging the finished apartments to showcase them to prospective tenants and investors. It soon became apparent that if the apartment was staged before viewing, it would be rented or sold a lot quicker than if it wasn't; sometimes even on the same day.

I had a eureka moment and founded my own property staging business, armed with all the expertise I had gathered. Since then, I have worked with hundreds of small property developers and homeowners, and seen time and time again the power and impact of making the right decisions from the start to transform investment properties; to increase kerb appeal and maximise their assets. Helping their properties sell quicker with a greater ROI has had a huge transformative shift on their lives – and the lives of other people – and I want to show you how you can do this, easily and well, too.

My grandfather was a successful entrepreneur, so I understood from an early age that it takes hard work, determination and a little bit of stubbornness to build a business. I guess that has always been in my blood. Through my businesses I've helped small property developers flourish, grow and become more business savvy. I have guided them into making the correct decisions when it comes to developing and flipping their properties, choosing the right finishes and presenting them to showcase a lifestyle to their target audience to get the greatest ROI.

Rather than the standard manual, *Flip and Fly* will show you an easy, practical process – a new way to think outside the box. I will explain how to avoid all the costly pitfalls and get you out of the frustrating 'limbo land' most developers find themselves in, draining all their finances and energy to prevent them from flying high. Having been in the same position in 2015, I can empathise with how it feels to be in this situation and the profound effect it had on my life and my health. I want to guide you through the minefield of buying, flipping and selling their properties to give you the financial freedom you dream of.

Flip and Fly will show you how to understand the property market, choose the right property and make the best ROI possible. It will give you all the knowledge to help you make informed decisions when flipping your property and market it to gain maximum kerb appeal. It will show you how to choose the right vendor that is suited to your property and market your property so it appeals to the widest possible audience, vastly increasing the probability of a sale in the quickest possible time.

This book has an extra level of creativity and thinking, which will be applied to the three key stages of flipping your property: buying, flipping and selling.

INTRODUCTION

1. Buying. In Part 1, I will explain how to research the property market and find properties that are undervalued or distressed, which can be bought for a lower price and renovated to increase their value. I'll demonstrate how to find the right property in the right location, which has potential for renovation and improvement and is priced below market value. I will guide you on how to set a budget and secure your finances and also offer advice on calculating the potential profits you can make from flipping your property sustainably.

2. Flipping. In Part 2, I will guide you through how to flip a property effectively to increase its value and appeal to your target demographic audience. I will help you understand which areas to focus on and which items give you the highest return on investment. I will also explain how to manage the job and create a streamline programme of works that will effectively deliver your project on time and within budget.

3. Selling. In Part 3, I will cover how to correctly showcase the property once it is flipped to get maximum kerb appeal. I will direct you on how to put it on the market and sell it for a profit, how to work with an estate agent to ensure that the property is priced correctly and marketed effectively, and how to grow your business effectively to give you the financial security to be able to enjoy life again.

This is the ultimate guide on how to make smart decisions in all aspects of flipping your investment property, which will guarantee the maximum ROI and a quick and easy sale so that you can fly high in the property development business. The book's hands-on approach and easy-to-follow guidelines will take you from finding the right property through to sealing the deal on a sale and beyond. I will show you all the steps to help you make a healthy profit and grow your property flipping business.

If you are a budding property entrepreneur, this is the guide for you; the book many successful developers wish they'd had when starting out. I will show you how to avoid all the pitfalls and share all the secrets of the savviest developers I know, enabling you to have the thriving, successful property flipping business that you have always dreamed of, giving you financial freedom to be able to start doing all the things you enjoy again. If you are buying, planning or building a property for investment, this book will help you grow fast, move on and flip and fly to the next level.

PART ONE
GETTING READY

1
What Is House Flipping And Why Is It For You?

Talk to many property investors today and as soon as they hear the two words: 'house flipping', their ears prick up. This is for good reason. Flipping can be big business when it comes to making a good profit quickly in the current property market.

The Finbri Property Flipping UK Report 2022[1] stated that over 62% of property flipped in the UK in the last two years made between £10K and 75K in profit. According to their survey, 31.57% of people's most recent property flips made between £10K and £25K profit; a combined 62.45% of flips made between £10K

---

1   Finbri, *Property Flipping UK Report 2022* (22 September 2022), https://finbri.co.uk/blog/property-flipping-uk-report-2022, accessed 11 October 2023

and £75K in profit; while only 6.29% broke even and just 1% of property flippers made a loss.

Interestingly, according to this Finbri report, the most popular type of property flipped in the UK over the last two years has been flats or apartments located in residential blocks (44.86%); more popular than those situated above shops or commercial units (18.28%). The second most-flipped type of property has been terraced houses (32.27%), ahead of semi-detached (26.87%) and detached (14.19%) properties.

Interestingly, also according to the same report, the recent increase in online searches for 'flipping houses' on Google is on the up. In July and August 2022, there were a combined 32K searches compared to the previous year's 18K, a year-on-year increase of over 77%. This indicates that more and more people are showing interest in flipping property.

The growth in house flipping can be attributed to several factors, including a shortage of homes for sale and an increase in demand for larger renovated homes. Additionally, the COVID-19 pandemic has prompted many people to re-evaluate their long-term living situations and work-life balance, leading to an increase in demand for homes and a rise in house prices in many areas.

With these figures in mind, there has never been a better time than now to start flipping and grab a piece of the pie in this fast-emerging market.

What is house flipping?

House flipping (the standard industry term for flipping residential property, including flats) refers to the practice of purchasing a property, renovating or upgrading it, and then reselling it for a profit.

The term 'flipping' indicates that, to maximise profits, the property needs to be sold quickly – speed is of the essence. The time it takes to flip an average two-bedroom house or flat successfully can vary enormously, depending on various factors such as the location and condition of the property, the extent of the renovation needed and the availability of contractors and materials. If the correct processes are followed, the average flip can take around six to eight months from start to finish. This ballpark timescale includes all the various stages – planning, purchasing, refurbishing and reselling – and is worth knowing as a benchmark for when you are planning your own property to flip.

Throughout the flipping process, there are many stages that need careful planning, due diligence and time investment, but all have equal importance on the success of your flip. I will discuss all the stages in more detail in the following chapters, but in brief:

- **The planning and purchasing stage** involves researching the local property market, identifying the most profitable areas to invest in and finding and negotiating the purchase of a suitable property.

- **The refurbishing stage** involves renovating and decorating the property to a good habitable standard, with a sustainable approach, within a given time frame.

- **The presentation and reselling stage** involves presenting the property to maximise its potential and appeal to the widest possible audience, finding a buyer and negotiating a sale to secure a successful ROI.

Flipping typically involves finding a property that is usually in need of repair or renovation, buying it at a low price, and then investing time and money in improving it. The goal is to make a profit on the spread between the purchase price and the sale price, minus the cost of repairs and renovations, and to make the sale for profit in a short space of time.

Flipping doesn't always rely on an uplift. In a hot market, you can sometimes get an absolute bargain at an auction house or through an estate agent – and also through off-market purchases at below-market valuation – and simply put the property back on the market and make yourself a nice 20K profit while hardly lifting a finger. In today's market, these bargains are rare, but they do come up and it's worth knowing how to spot them when they do.

WHAT IS HOUSE FLIPPING AND WHY IS IT FOR YOU?

In most cases, a property in a bad state of repair will need work and money thrown at it to make it habitable or – even better – more desirable, with more kerb appeal than a similar property down the road.

Working quickly is the key. The quicker you flip, the higher the ROI. A property that is standing empty after renovation or upgrading, or waiting for work to be done, is incurring costs, which can often include:

- **Property taxes:** In most places, council tax is still due on a vacant property. This can be a significant expense, depending on the value of the property and the local tax rates. It can increase significantly for empty properties after a specified period (depending on the local authority).

- **Insurance:** Property insurance can often be higher for vacant properties because of the increased risk of damage or theft. Even though the property is empty, it is still necessary to protect the property against theft, fire and other risks.

- **Community charges:** These apply if the property is in an apartment block with a communal hallway requiring cleaning and maintenance.

- **Utilities:** Depending on the local regulations and the property's set-up, the owner may be responsible for maintaining certain utilities such as water, gas and electricity.

- **Security:** Vacant properties are often at a higher risk of vandalism, theft and other crimes. As a result, the owner may need to invest in additional security measures, such as alarm systems and security cameras.

Flipping to sell or rent

Before you start looking for a property or even narrowing down the area you want to search in, you need to identify your end user. This will be determined by whether you are selling to refinance another purchase or renting to generate a steady income after completion.

Likely candidates for flipping will fit into two main categories: buy to sell and buy to hold.

Buy to sell (if you are selling at completion)

Buy to sell is a process in which you purchase a property with the intention of selling it for a profit. This may involve minor or major cosmetic improvements to make the property habitable, or no improvements at all. The property is typically sold within a set period of time – often within a few months – with the goal to make a profit by increasing the property's value and maximising its kerb appeal.

House flipping is a more aggressive version of buy to sell, with timescale being the key component. This is where you purchase a property that needs repairs or renovations, make those improvements and then sell the property for a profit. House flippers often aim to complete the renovations as quickly as possible to minimise holding costs and maximise profits, taking advantage of a good market, low purchase price or other favourable conditions.

Buy to hold (if you are renting the property at completion)

This strategy involves purchasing a property that needs improvements, making those improvements and then refinancing the property to take advantage of its increased value. The goal is to increase the property's value through renovations and then use the increased equity to obtain financing for future investments. These investments are often used for either long-term rentals to tenants or Airbnb/holiday rentals (short-term rentals).

Long-term rentals generate a regular income but often require a lot more hands-on management and maintenance to ensure rent payments are met and any maintenance issues are dealt with swiftly. The owner needs to comply with regularly updated legislation, such as EPC ratings and building regulations, and the properties can sometimes be costly to maintain and bring up to current standards.

Airbnb/holiday rentals (short-term rentals) also need ongoing hands-on management to deal with regular changeovers of guests, cleaning and maintenance. Properties with higher rental values and holiday homes also require higher-grade finishes. These, however, tend to generate a higher rental yield income than long-term rentals, but on a more sporadic or seasonal basis. It is worth bearing in mind when working through your finance structure when you will need financial buffers in place to see you over the drier periods.

That flippin' house: Understanding your 'why', mission and vision

As well as understanding the intended outcome from your property flip, when starting any business, it's vital to understand your personal motivation – your 'why' (literally, why are you doing this?). Your 'why' will give you a sense of purpose, direction and motivation when times get tough – and in property flipping, times are guaranteed to get tough at some point.

You might have been developing property as a hobby for some time or have fallen into doing so because of a windfall or inheritance. If you want to accelerate your interest into a successful business, you need to start from first business principles and consider your 'why'.

Your 'why' represents your deeper reason for starting your business, and it can help guide your decision making, inspire your team and attract buyers and investors who share your values.

Keeping your 'why' in mind, in whatever you set out to do, is an extremely powerful tool and even more so when starting your property flipping business. Why…? Because *you* are your greatest resource. We need to start at the foundations of you, as your business's success is relying heavily on your energy and motivation.

Take some time to think about your 'why' and what you want to get out of your property developing business. It can be the ultimate key to your success.

Your 'why' could be one of the following:

- **Providing financial freedom** so that you can eventually free up your time to do the things you enjoy: spending more time with the family, going on more holidays or buying your own dream home.

- **Having a financially secure future** so that you can retire earlier than you would in a nine-to-five job.

- **Wanting a more flexible day-to-day schedule**, for example to be able to watch your kids in the school concert without having to ask your boss for time off.

- **A wider social purpose** such as increasing the pool of attractive, affordable, sustainable housing in a run-down neighbourhood.

Understanding your 'why' helps you to define your mission and vision. These should represent the problem you're solving or the value you're providing to your end users (your buyers or tenants). When you're clear on your mission and vision, you can start to create a strong business plan and strategy that aligns with those goals. We will explore the business plan in more depth in the next chapter.

Your 'why' also helps you to make decisions. When you're faced with tough decisions, you can use your 'why' to guide your choices. If your 'why' is to improve people's lives, for example, you might prioritise product features that are most impactful for your buyers, such as developing for social housing or creating houses with a zero-carbon footprint.

Your 'why' can also attract buyers. When you can clearly articulate your 'why', it can help you differentiate your business from competitors and attract buyers who share your values. Buyers and tenants are often attracted to developers that stand for something and are making a positive impact on the world.

A clear mission and vision are essential ingredients in any successful business. They help to identify the purpose of your business – both present and future – and set the direction for growth. They provide a clear picture of where your business is going in the future. Having this clarity of direction helps you to drill down on the goals, strategies and actions needed to get it there. They can also be used to differentiate the business from its competitors and create its own USP.

Your mission is the next step or milestone to achieve the vision. It is a brief statement that outlines the business's core purpose, its primary services and its target audience. It communicates the reason why the business exists and what it aims to achieve. A well-crafted mission statement provides a sense of direction and purpose for the business, guiding decision making and helping to align investors towards the business's goal. It is generally focused on the present and outlines the business's current purpose.

Your vision is your ultimate goal for your business. It is a statement of the business's aspirations for the future and describes the long-term goal that the business wants to achieve. It is usually more inspirational and abstract than a mission statement and sets out the big picture of what the business wants to become. The vision statement is usually future-oriented and outlines the company's aspirations and goals for the future.

Both your mission and vision statements can serve as strong benchmarks for your business and help you to evaluate its performance. It can be a clear indication to assess whether it is meeting its objectives and making progress towards its vision.

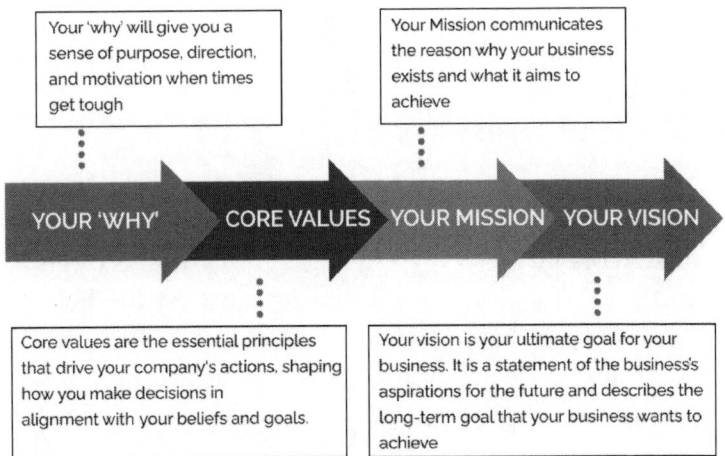

The 4-step foundations to success

KEEP THE FINISH LINE IN SIGHT

When I'm not writing books or staging properties my passion is ultra running, mainly in the hills. This often involves running long distances, sometimes over a few days with little sleep.

The build-up to these events and the pre-event training schedules are intense. The starting line is where imposter syndrome kicks in. That is when I need to bring in the 'why': 'Why am I here? What am I doing? Why am I doing this?' I always make sure I have the finish line set in my mind from the outset. If I don't, I know I won't reach the end.

Ultra running, by its nature, is a journey of often-extreme highs and lows: the highs being the checkpoints where you can fuel up with jelly babies and a hearty stew and take a short rest, and of course the finish line; the lows being when your body is hurting with every inch of its being and you are so tired you are almost falling asleep on your feet. To get through the lows, I literally have to remember why I am there, what I am doing and why I am doing it. This is an extremely powerful tool that has got me past the points where I wanted to quit right there, right then. It has forced me to focus on the greater goal of what I want to achieve and has given me the motivation to keep going, whatever was thrown at me along the way. In ultra running, this is usually a good dose of torrential rain and mud!

Why this business isn't for softies

Let's be clear about this. Property flipping can be hard work and labour intensive. It involves a wide range of tasks, from identifying undervalued properties and securing financing to managing renovation projects effectively and marketing the property for sale.

Flippers must be able to work under tight timelines and manage project budgets carefully to ensure that they are able to make a profit. Additionally, renovating a property can be physically demanding. Flippers may need to work long hours to complete the necessary renovations – often late into the evenings and at weekends if you are fitting your flipping project around a day job and planning to do some (or all) of the work yourself. Property flipping can also be risky as the market can be unpredictable and there may be unforeseen costs associated with renovating a property. Flippers need to be able to manage these risks and make decisions quickly to ensure that they are able to turn a profit.

That said, property flipping can also be an extremely rewarding and profitable venture for those who are able to do it successfully. With the right skills and expertise, property flippers can turn a run-down property into a desirable home and make a profit in the process.

What do most of the developers I have worked with wish they'd known early on? Having a clear understanding of the development process and all the skillsets involved is crucial if you want to make your business a success. This will enable you to delegate effectively further down the line, but on your first couple of flips it pays to be fully hands-on to understand what works and what doesn't. If you are just starting out, I would always recommend working on one property at a time until you fully understand the process, which we will explore in later chapters.

While house flipping can be a challenging and risky endeavour, careful planning and preparation can make it a lucrative investment opportunity. Don't be in that one per cent of flippers whose flip flops for lack of understanding upfront.

2
The Developer's Mindset

Flipping a property requires a lot more than just buying low and selling high. To be successful, you must have a developer's mindset, which means approaching the property as a project that requires careful planning, execution and management.

This chapter will explore the importance of how having a good developer's mindset can help you avoid common mistakes and maximise your profits. We will discuss the key principles of a developer's mindset, such as having a clear vision, being proactive and being adaptable.

Additionally, we will delve into the specific skills and qualities that are necessary for a successful property flip, including budgeting, time management, communication, sustainability and problem-solving. By the end of this chapter, you will have a thorough understanding of what it means to have a developer's mindset and how to apply it to your own property flipping endeavours for greater success.

It's not about you: The business mindset

It's easy to fall into the trap of renovating a house with your own personal tastes at the forefront of your mind. Many new developers do this, and I did it myself when I renovated my rental flat in Leeds and put it on the market a few years ago. I had been a professional interior designer for twenty-five years, so surely my tastes would match with those of the wider demographic audience I was aiming towards? Unfortunately, I learned pretty fast that this was not the case.

If you know what you like (as I do), it is tempting to think that by planning the property upgrade to suit your own tastes and needs you will appeal to the mass market that you ultimately want to sell to. Perhaps on first walking into your property you had an appealing vision of the end result that led you to make the purchase. You had formed an emotional attachment based on how much you would like the property, and in my experience this is the opposite of what works.

To become a successful property flipper and make a good living out of it, your first task is to shift your mindset from that of someone buying a property for their own enjoyment to that of a business. Your goal is not to create the perfect home for yourself but to build a successful property development business that will eventually lead you to financial freedom.

With this in mind, you need to shift your focus to the end user's tastes and needs in every decision you make, including the design process and layout, selection of materials and finishing touches. This is important for several reasons.

Meeting the needs of the market

Many of the successful developers I work with have a clear understanding of catering to the preferences and needs of their end users to ensure that their properties are in line with market demand. This will increase the appeal of your properties to potential buyers or tenants, and help you generate greater interest and demand for your projects.

Large developers such as Bellway Homes capture this perfectly. They invest a large amount of time and money researching local target demographic appeal. If you can visit their show homes and look at their floor plans of a similar sized property to yours, these can be a great source for inspiration and insight into the sorts of homes that people want to buy in that particular area.

Maximising profitability

By developing properties that meet the needs of the end users, you will be able to yield higher prices or rental rates, which will increase your profitability. Additionally, properties that are more appealing to the market are likely to sell or rent more quickly, which can reduce your holding costs and hugely increase your return on investment.

Reducing risk

By flipping properties that meet the needs of the end users, you will reduce the risk of holding on to properties that don't meet market demand. This will help to minimise the risk of having your property standing vacant or having low occupancy rates, and help you avoid potential losses.

There is no use in flipping a four-bedroom family home when the nearest good school is twenty miles away and there is no parking available. Similarly, city-based properties are usually better suited to younger professionals who commute by bike or public transport, so parking is probably not on their list of priorities.

What do successful flippers do?

The most successful property developers I have worked with over the years have shared a similar mindset in the ways in which they approach the process of identifying, acquiring and developing property with the goal of creating value and generating a profit. Here are some of their key characteristics:

- **Having a good vision:** They can see a property's potential beyond its current condition and imagine what it could become with the right investment and development.

- **Creative thinking:** They think outside the box and come up with innovative solutions to challenges.

- **Risk taking:** Successful property development is inherently risky as it involves investing sometimes large amounts of money in a property that may or may not generate a profit. There may be changes in market conditions, construction delays and unexpected expenses. A good property developer's mindset involves the ability to manage these risks well by conducting thorough research, creating contingency plans and making strategic decisions. The most successful flippers are willing to take calculated risks and make informed decisions based on their knowledge and experience.

- **Patience:** Property development is a complex, time-consuming process that requires patience and a long-term perspective. Being able to stay focused on goals and see the project through to completion, even in the face of challenges or setbacks, is definitely an attribute to them being successful.

- **Good financial acumen:** They all have a deep understanding of the financial aspects of their developments, including financing, budgeting and profit margins. Being able to analyse and manage financial risk and make decisions based on their understanding of the financial implications of their choices has had a huge effect on their success as property developers.

- **Ability to identify profitable investment opportunities:** This includes understanding market trends, analysing property values and identifying areas with growth potential. With this knowledge, they can make informed decisions that maximise their profits.

- **Understanding how to maximise the value of a property:** This includes identifying potential improvements that can increase the property's value, such as upgrading the kitchen, adding an extra room or incorporating a sustainable approach to design and construction. By identifying these improvements, they can increase the value of the property and maximise their profits.

- **Embracing a sustainable approach:** This can significantly boost the value of the property in several compelling ways. By incorporating energy-efficient appliances, solar panels and insulation upgrades, the property's overall energy performance improves, leading to lower utility costs for future occupants. The use of eco-friendly materials and water-saving fixtures not only promotes environmental consciousness but also appeals to buyers seeking a reduced ecological footprint and lower operational expenses.

- **Building relationships:** Having the ability to build strong relationships with contractors, suppliers and other industry professionals can lead to cost savings and better-quality work, which help increase profitability.

CASE STUDY: See the potential and reap the rewards

An experienced property flipper with whom I have worked for many years recently came across a neglected Victorian-era house in a charming neighbourhood on the outskirts of Manchester. While others saw it as a dilapidated structure, he saw beyond its current condition and envisioned its transformation into a stunning family home.

As he stepped into the house, he immediately recognised the property's unique architectural features, such as the intricate woodwork, high ceilings and original fireplace. He could visualise the house restored to its former glory, blending modern comforts with the historic charm that attracted buyers to the area.

With a keen eye for design, sustainability and a deep understanding of buyer preferences, he crafted a vision for the property and imagined an extensive renovation that would preserve the character-defining elements while incorporating modern upgrades. He envisioned an open floor plan, a bright and airy kitchen and upgraded bathrooms that would appeal to discerning buyers seeking a blend of old-world charm and contemporary amenities.

To bring his vision to life, he assembled a team of skilled contractors, architects and designers who shared his passion for restoring historic properties. Together, they developed a detailed renovation plan that included restoring original features, salvaging and repurposing materials from the original structure whenever possible to reduce waste and lower renovation costs, repairing structural issues and enhancing the property's functionality and aesthetics.

He was mindful of the market demand and the neighbourhood's appeal to families. With this in mind, he envisioned creating a welcoming outdoor space, complete with a landscaped garden, a patio and a children's play area. He believed that transforming the backyard into a functional and attractive space would further elevate the property's appeal.

Throughout the renovation process, he maintained a clear vision and worked closely with his team, ensuring that every decision aligned with his goal of creating a dream family home. He carefully selected good-quality materials, fixtures and finishes that would showcase the property's character and enhance its market value.

Once the renovation was complete, the once-neglected Victorian house was transformed into a stunning, move-in-ready residence. His vision, attention to detail and understanding of the market allowed him to create a property that stood out among the competition. The house sold quickly, with the assistance of our property staging, and at a premium price, exceeding both the buyer's expectations and the neighbourhood's standards.

His success as a property flipper stemmed from his ability to see beyond the property's current condition and imagine its potential. His vision, combined with his expertise in renovation and market trends, allowed him to create a desirable home that maximised the property's value and appealed to buyers seeking a unique blend of historic charm and modern living.

Changing your mindset to that of a savvy property developer to focus on the end user's tastes and needs can be challenging for a newbie starting out, but here are some useful steps that can help:

- **Research your target market:** Before embarking on a property development project, it's important to research your target market and understand their preferences, needs and lifestyles. This can involve analysing demographic data, carrying out surveys and studying trends in the local property market.
- **Engage with potential buyers/tenants:** Do this early in the development process to get feedback

on their preferences and needs. This can involve attending networking groups, conducting surveys or using social media outreach to gather input and insights. Estate and letting agents can also offer some great nuggets of knowledge at this stage.

- **Stay up to date with design trends and best practices in property development:** Incorporate these into your plans where appropriate. This can help ensure that your properties are attractive and appealing to a wide range of buyers or tenants.

CASE STUDY: Be prepared to pivot for success

A developer we recently worked with flipped a three-bedroom bungalow in The Wirral. He purchased the property for £277,500. After spending £80,000 on renovations, he sold it for £550,000, giving him a 35% profit in just 7.5 months from start to completion of works – keeping holding costs to a minimum and being able to maximise on his overall profit. A rare find these days you may think, but this example proves that if you have your end user in mind throughout the whole flip process, outstanding results are much more likely to happen.

The surrounding area had good schools with great Ofsted reports, local shops and amenities and a health centre. The area was clearly perfect for young families – but the house was a bungalow with a relatively small lounge, and didn't quite suit the young family market.

Instead, he decided to target the flip towards a couple in their mid-sixties looking at downsizing and being closer to grandchildren. The finishes used were of a high spec with tasteful neutral decor and a well-designed kitchen/dining area. When we staged the property prior to putting it on the market, we focused the furniture and accessories to appeal to this particular target market.

The success of this flip was down to the developer firmly understanding the end user at the start of the project and basing all his decisions around this. He thought one step beyond the standard family house set-up to include the grandparents who wanted a tasteful newly renovated home close to their grandchildren.

Many investors will tell you the potential for this size of profit is over, but this is a clear example that thinking outside the box can still yield opportunities.

Making a business plan

A strong business plan is the backbone of every successful property developer. It provides a good road map for your business and helps you to plan, prioritise and track your progress.

If you are creating a business from a hobby, it may be that in the past you have ad libbed from one DIY renovation to the next. This will not be enough to start building a profitable business, which requires careful planning from the onset. If you want a rewarding, exciting career in property flipping, it is important to take the time to establish a solid business foundation from the start.

Overall, you will need a solid financial plan, well-structured business goals and a good action plan. To help get you started, first you need to consider:

- **The end use of most of your properties:** Buy and flip to let or buy and flip to sell, as we discussed in the previous chapter.
- **Your USP:** How you will stand out from other developers in your area.
- **Your aims and goals:** Where you want to be in five, ten and twenty years. This is crucial for not getting sidetracked from your end goals.

Your business plan should detail your business, your target market and how you plan to attract them, and projected expenses and income. You can download a free business plan template from the government website.[2]

It might also be a good idea to hire a financial adviser to help you put together a forecast that will guide your business for the short, medium and long term. Having over-ambitious or under-ambitious financial forecasts (watch *Dragons' Den* for examples of both) can put a potential investor off immediately, as it

---

2   GOV.UK, 'Write a Business Plan', https://gov.uk/write-business-plan, accessed 11 October 2023

shows you don't have good knowledge of the optics of the business.

A good business plan will help you raise finances, if needed. Many mortgage lenders will ask for a business plan to help give them confidence that you have a good asset for them to invest in. It will also help you plan how your business will expand, increasing the likelihood that it will succeed. It is worth noting that a business plan is a live document and should be updated periodically to always stay current.

What should be in your business plan?

Here are the key components you will need to include. You can add the information or sections as you work through the relevant chapters in this book.

- **Executive summary:** A brief overview of your property flipping business plan, including your mission statement, goals and objectives.

- **Market analysis:** A thorough analysis of the property market in the areas where you plan to flip properties. This includes demographic information, economic data and analysis of local property values, trends and competition.

- **Business model:** An explanation of your property flipping business model, including your target market, property acquisition strategy, renovation and marketing plans, and expected profit margins.

- **Property acquisition strategy:** An outline of how you will acquire properties, including your criteria for selecting properties, sources of funding and negotiation tactics.

- **Renovation plan:** A detailed description of your renovation plan, including your budget, timeline, renovation team and expected ROI.

- **Marketing plan:** An overview of your marketing strategy, including how you will price and promote your flipped properties and how you will reach potential buyers.

- **Financial projections:** A realistic projection of your financial performance, including your start-up costs, operating expenses, revenue projections and profit margins.

- **Your team:** An introduction to your team, including their experience, qualifications and roles and responsibilities within your business.

- **Risk assessment:** A list of potential risks and challenges that your property flipping business may face, and your plans to mitigate them.

- **Exit strategy:** An explanation of your exit strategy is key as it provides a clear goal for the business owner to work towards. It helps to define the end game and the steps that need to be taken to achieve it, including an outline of the timeline, how you will value your business when it comes time to exit, and the different exit options you are considering, such as selling the business or merging with another company.

By including all these elements, you can create a comprehensive roadmap that will guide your business through the start-up phase and beyond.

A SAMPLE BUSINESS PLAN

Executive summary

The property flipping business aims to purchase properties at a lower price, renovate them and sell them at a higher price for profit. Our company will focus on single-family homes in desirable neighbourhoods. Our team consists of experienced property developing professionals, contractors and designers.

Market analysis

The real estate market in our target area is growing and demand for homes is increasing. Our analysis shows that there are a large number of properties in need of renovation in our target neighbourhoods. Our goal is to identify undervalued properties with high potential for renovation, add value through upgrades and sell them for a profit.

Marketing strategy

We plan to market our properties through various channels, including social media, email marketing and traditional print advertisements. We will also work with local real estate agents to find potential buyers for our properties. We aim to create a strong brand presence in the market by showcasing our renovations through before and after photos and emphasising our attention to detail.

Operations plan

We will focus on acquiring distressed properties at a discount, negotiating favourable terms with contractors and managing the renovation process efficiently. We will also maintain a close relationship with local building departments to ensure that our renovations are up to code. We plan to hire an experienced project manager to oversee the renovation process and ensure that each project stays on schedule and within budget.

Financial plan

Our financial goal is to achieve a 25% ROI for each property. We plan to use a combination of cash and financing to purchase properties, with a target acquisition cost of 70% of the after-repair value. We will budget for renovation costs based on the scope of work and hire contractors and designers who can deliver quality work within budget. We will also factor in selling costs, including real estate agent commissions and closing costs.

Conclusion

The property flipping business is a profitable venture that requires careful planning, market analysis and strong project management skills. With our experienced team, strategic marketing plan and careful financial planning, we are confident in our ability to achieve our goal of flipping properties for profit.

Understand your tasks

We will go into more detail in the coming chapters, but here is a brief outline of the key tasks you will need to complete for a successful flip, and the order in which they need to be done:

1. **Identify a property:** Find a property that is undervalued or in need of significant improvement. This could involve searching online property listings, attending auctions or working with an estate agent.

2. **Conduct due diligence:** Before purchasing a property, you will need to ensure that it is a good investment. This could involve researching the local property market, conducting a property inspection and estimating the costs of renovations.

3. **Secure financing:** You may use your own funds to purchase a property or secure financing from a bank or private lender. Financing options may include a traditional mortgage, a bridging loan, a line of credit or a hard money loan.

4. **Renovate the property:** Once the property is purchased, you will begin renovating or improving it. This could involve light cosmetic changes like painting and landscaping, or more significant renovations like replacing electrical and plumbing systems or adding additional square meterage.

5. **Manage the project budget:** Throughout the flipping process, you will need to manage your budget carefully to ensure that you are able to make a profit. This will involve tracking expenses and making decisions about where to allocate resources.

6. **Market and sell the property:** Once the renovations are complete, you will stage the property and list it for sale. This may involve working with a professional property stager and an estate agent or conducting your own marketing efforts.

7. **Close the sale:** Once a buyer is found and a purchase agreement is reached, you will close the sale and collect your profits.

Who can help you?

Certain professionals are extremely useful, if not indispensable, depending on the nature and scale of your project. We will look at their roles in more depth in Part 2, but most developers I have worked with all work with the following specialists to get the pre-project prep up and running successfully:

- **Project manager:** Saves you time, stress and money by planning, scheduling and coordinating the various elements of a construction project and ensuring completion is within budget and on time. They troubleshoot day-to-day on-site issues.

- **Quantity surveyor:** Drives the budget of the project, managing costs and risks and negotiating with suppliers, contractors and stakeholders to ensure high quality. Like the project manager, they are well worth the investment for the difference they will make to your stress levels and profitability.

- **Structural engineer:** Ensures compliance and safety for extensive renovations that need to pass building controls, such as an internal remodelling or extension.

- **Architect:** Helps you create a design that maximises the potential of a property, attracts your target market and ensures a higher ROI.

Summary

- Having a good property developer's mindset is essential for making a profit in property development.

- Understanding the market is crucial to identify opportunities and make informed decisions.

- Managing risks effectively helps mitigate potential setbacks and protect your investment.

- Maximising property value through strategic renovations, sustainable upgrades and improvements can increase profitability.

- Building strong relationships with stakeholders, such as contractors, suppliers and investors, can lead to favourable deals and partnerships.

- Making informed decisions based on market research and analysis helps maximise overall profits.

- Continuously staying up to date on market trends and industry insights is important for making profitable decisions.

- Adopting a proactive and adaptable approach allows for quick adjustments to market conditions and emerging opportunities.

- Emphasising long-term profitability over short-term gains ensures sustainable success in property development.

- Developing financial literacy and understanding the financial aspects of property development is key to maximising profits.

3
The Property Market

The property market is complex and dynamic. Understanding it is essential for anyone looking to enter the world of property flipping, as it allows investors to make informed decisions about where and when to invest their money.

This chapter will explore the various aspects of the property market, including market trends, supply and demand, and economic indicators, which can impact the success of a property flip. Additionally, it will highlight the importance of conducting thorough research and analysis of the property market to mitigate risks and maximise profits in property flipping.

By providing a comprehensive understanding of the property market, this chapter will equip you with the knowledge and tools necessary to navigate the industry and make strategic investment decisions that will help you achieve success in property flipping and build a profitable portfolio of properties over time.

Understanding the market

The housing property market can be complex and subject to various economic and social factors, sometimes making it challenging to predict and understand in any given climate.

Whether you have acquired a property through an inheritance or are about to start looking for your own property to buy and flip, there are many key market-related factors to take into account in order for you to maximise your investment. Having an understanding of the housing property market in any climate requires consideration of factors including:

- **Supply and demand:** The relationship between supply and demand has a crucial role in determining the housing property market's performance. If there is a shortage of housing supply in a particular area, it can lead to a rise in property prices as demand increases. Conversely, if there is an oversupply of housing, it can lead to a fall in prices.
- **Interest rates:** These can significantly impact the housing property market. Low interest rates can

make borrowing money cheaper, leading to an increase in demand for housing, which can drive up prices. Conversely, higher interest rates can deter buyers from taking out a mortgage, leading to a decrease in demand for housing.

- **Economic conditions:** The strength of the economy can have a significant impact on the housing property market. During periods of economic growth and stability, there is often an increase in employment rates and consumer confidence, leading to a rise in property prices. Conversely, during economic downturns, unemployment rates may increase and consumer confidence may decrease, leading to a fall in property prices.

- **Legislation:** Government legislation, including tax incentives, stamp duty and regulations such as EPC changes for landlords, can have a significant impact on the housing property market. For example, tax breaks for first-time buyers or incentives for property developers can stimulate demand for housing and lead to a rise in property prices. On the other hand, regulations on property development or taxes on property transactions can reduce demand and lead to a fall in property prices.

- **Demographics:** Demographic factors such as population growth and age distribution can also have an effect on the housing property market. An increase in the population or migration to a particular area can lead to a rise in demand for housing, driving up prices. Conversely, an ageing population may result in a decrease in demand for housing, leading to a fall in prices.

Recessions and booms in the property market

Recessions and booms in the property market are periods of economic and market activity where the demand for property is either weak or strong.

A recession occurs when the economy as a whole experiences a downturn, resulting in reduced demand for property. In such times, property values may decline and repossessions tend to rise. This situation is often influenced by factors like high unemployment rates, diminished consumer confidence and limited access to credit.

A boom in the property market happens when there is a surge in demand for property. During a property market boom, property values escalate and there is typically a substantial number of sales and new construction projects. This upswing is typically driven by low interest rates, robust employment rates and heightened consumer confidence.

Both property market recessions and booms can have significant effects on the overall economy. For instance, during a property market boom there is increased economic activity, including job creation and higher spending levels. There are also associated risks such as overbuilding or the formation of a housing bubble, which can subsequently trigger a significant downturn.

While a property boom may look more attractive to property flippers, it can also lead to over-investment and eventually result in a property crash. A property recession may present buying opportunities, but it can also lead to negative equity and reduced confidence in the property market. Make sure you weigh up the pros and cons of both scenarios to be able to make a calculated decision based on the current economic climate and how it can work best for you.

Understanding your ceiling price

The ceiling price of a property is the highest amount that a similar size and type of property in the same area or street can be sold for when renovated. The ceiling price is the backbone of every successful property developer's business plan and must be defined before you even start the process of making an offer or bid at an auction house. Being able to calculate the ceiling price before you buy a property will determine how much you want to pay for it and how much profit you can make after flipping.

In simple terms:

> Ceiling price − renovation costs − profit margin = purchase price

How to calculate a realistic ceiling price

To calculate your ceiling price, check the recent sales prices of properties similar to yours on the same street or nearby. Zoopla (www.zoopla.co.uk) is probably the best portal to use to find this information as it outlines the history of purchases on any given property.

Ask yourself the following questions to get a like-for-like comparison:

- Is the property detached, semi-detached or terraced? A flat in a managed block? A converted flat?
- How big is the garden, if it has one?
- What condition is the property in?
- Has an extension been added to the property? Could similar work be done on yours?
- Has there been a recent addition of a new school/supermarket/transport network to the area?

The pandemic had a huge impact on the relative importance of the location of properties in perception of value. Fifty of the biggest UK employers have said that they have no plans to return all staff to the office full time in the near future.[3] Cities and well-connected suburbs were once the most desirable places for office workers to live for accessibility and shorter commutes, but that is not necessarily the case in post-pandemic society.

Building communities while property flipping

Building communities is important as it fosters positive relationships with residents, contributes to the neighbourhood's overall well-being and identity, and creates a sense of pride and belonging among community members by integrating thoughtful strategies to positively impact the neighbourhood and foster strong connections with residents. Here's how to do this while flipping your property:

- **Reach out to the existing community:** Listen to the concerns, ideas and needs of neighbours, local businesses and community organisations. Involve them in the decision-making process for the project.

---

3   S Jack, 'No plan for a return to the office for millions of staff', *BBC News* (26 August 2022), www.bbc.co.uk/news/business-53901310, accessed 7 November 2023

- **Strive to maintain the neighbourhood's architectural character:** Respecting the area's historical elements and aesthetics helps to preserve its identity and contributes to a cohesive community.

- **Identify and address specific needs within the community:** If there is a lack of affordable housing, focus on providing accessible, reasonably priced units.

- **Maintain open and transparent communication with the community:** Keep residents informed during all stages about the project's timeline, potential disruptions and any benefits it might bring to the area.

- **Use local contractors, suppliers and vendors:** This supports the local economy and establishes a positive relationship between your business and the community.

- **Incorporate eco-friendly and sustainable design elements:** Demonstrating a commitment to environmental responsibility, such as including energy-efficient appliances or green building materials, can resonate with the community and potential buyers.

- **Host community events or workshops related to home improvement, design or sustainability:** These provide an opportunity to connect with residents and share knowledge, while also building goodwill.

By adopting these community-focused approaches, you can contribute positively to the neighbourhoods you work in, creating a lasting impact and building strong relationships with local residents.

Summary

- Having an understanding of the property market is paramount for anyone involved in property development. A comprehensive understanding of market trends, consumer preferences and economic factors is crucial for making informed decisions and maximising ROI.

- By closely monitoring market conditions, you can identify potential opportunities and accurately assess risks.

- Tailoring projects to meet the evolving demands of buyers or tenants is essential for success.

- Anticipating shifts in supply and demand allows for adjustments in pricing strategies.

- Effectively positioning projects in the competitive landscape is crucial.

- Staying attuned to the property market ensures the ability to navigate uncertainties.

- Capitalising on emerging trends is possible with market awareness.

- Optimising chances of success in the dynamic world of property development requires understanding the property market.

- Continuously staying informed about market trends is key to making strategic decisions.

- Building communities while property flipping is important.

4
Finding Your Investment Property

Finding the right investment property is one of the most important stages of flipping a property. Choosing the wrong property can lead to financial loss and a multitude of headaches, while the right property can be the key to a successful and profitable flip.

This chapter will explore the importance of finding the right property when flipping successfully, and how to identify properties with the most potential for a successful flip. We will examine the different factors to consider when searching for investment properties, such as location, condition and market trends. We will also discuss the various resources and tools available to help you find and evaluate potential investment properties, such as estate agents, online listings and property management companies. By the end of this chapter, you will have a comprehensive understanding of how to find the right investment property for your flipping ventures, setting you up for success in your property investments.

Finding a good property to flip involves a combination of research, analysis and strategy. Steps such as identifying your target market, researching the current property market, being on the lookout for distressed properties, being able to analyse the potential profit, considering the location, and building a network of estate agents, contractors and other professionals who can help you find properties that are not on the market, are all part of the process. These individuals can provide valuable advice and support throughout the flipping process.

It requires patience, attention to detail and a strategic approach, but by following the steps in this chapter you can increase your chances of finding a property that is suitable for flipping and can yield a healthy profit.

Auctions

How they work

Buying a property at auction can feel daunting as a first timer. Being fully prepared before you attend an auction will help the process run smoothly and give you the confidence to become an auction pro in no time. These steps will give you the valuable tools to do this:

1. **Research:** Before attending an auction, make sure you research the properties that will be up for sale. This includes conducting a title search to ensure that the property has a clear title, as well as inspecting the property to identify any potential issues or repairs that may be needed. You can obtain title searches from UK Land Register (https://uklandregister.co.uk). It is good practice to review any legal documents at this stage, which could have hidden costs associated and negatively affect any potential profit.

2. **Financing:** Auctions usually require bidders to have proof of financing, such as a pre-approval letter from a lender or proof of funds, if paying in cash. Always secure financing in advance of the auction to be prepared to bid on the property.

3. **Bidding:** On the day of the auction, attendees will typically register and receive a bidder number. Bidding typically starts at a certain amount and continues until there is only one bidder left. This can be competitive and fast-paced, and you may be bidding against experienced investors or other interested parties. Always have your highest price in your head and, however tempting it may be, don't go above this. Remember, this is your business and you need to think with your head, not your heart.

4. **Winning the bid:** If you win the bid, you will be required to put down a deposit on the property immediately; usually a percentage of the purchase price. The balance of the purchase price is usually due within a set time frame, usually within thirty to sixty days.

Before deciding to buy a house to flip at an auction house, it's worth noting the pros and cons of taking this route to acquire your property.

Pros

- **Lower prices:** Properties at auction houses are often sold at a lower price than their market value. This can be due to the condition of the property, seller motivation when houses may be owned by a bank or government agency, and time constraints when properties must be sold within a specific time frame. This time constraint can lead to a lower price because buyers are aware that the seller is motivated to sell the property quickly and may be willing to accept a lower price. This means that you may be able to get a good deal on a property that you can then flip and sell for a profit.

- **Quick purchase:** Auction houses often have a fast turnaround time for purchasing properties, which means you are able to secure the property quickly and start working on it almost right away.

- **Potential for high returns:** If you're able to purchase a property at a low price and then make strategic renovations and improvements, you can potentially sell the property for a much higher price and make a good profit.

Cons

- **High competition:** Auctions can be highly competitive, with many other investors bidding on the same properties. This can drive prices above the market value, making it more difficult to get a good deal.

- **Limited information:** When you buy a property at an auction house, you often have limited information about the property's condition and history. This can make it difficult to accurately assess the potential risks and rewards of a purchase.

- **Unknown repair costs:** Properties at auction houses are often sold 'as is', which means you may not know about all the repairs and renovations that will be required until after you've purchased the property. This can make it difficult to accurately estimate your total costs and potential profits. Often more expensive than a private treaty sale, this was the case especially during Covid with many cash-rich retail buyers paying way above what they would have paid via a private treaty.

Auction tips

Henry Davis, presenter of property refurbishment on behalf of the National Residential Landlords Association, gives these golden nuggets of information to bear in mind regarding auctions:

- The vendors' solicitor has no obligation to respond to any legal enquiries.

- Missing information in the legal pack is common. Most properties won't have a sellers' information pack.

- Out-of-date title documents can deliberately mislead on potential charges or notices.

- Deliberately temporarily repaired 'botch jobs' to hide greater problems like major cracks or subsidence are common.

- Unless you are highly experienced, you will struggle to have enough time to do the necessary due diligence. It is difficult to do due diligence with a rushed viewing.

- There is also not enough time to understand title covenants and get insurance advice to underwrite the covenant risk.

- Extra 'hidden' fees can occur, if you don't read all information in great detail.

- Fear of missing out (FOMO) is the norm, which leads to bidding wars and paying way over market value.

- Deliberately misleading low guide prices and sharp practice is standard in the industry.

- Unpaid management (usually not disclosed) fees on a leasehold are the responsibility of the new owner.

Many of the property flippers I work with often buy their houses at auction. It can be a good option if you are prepared and have done your research, but it may not be easy and it can involve risks and challenges. It is helpful to consult an estate agent or legal professional who has experience with property auctions to ensure that you fully understand the process and are prepared for any potential issues.

Property portals

How they work

Rightmove (www.rightmove.co.uk) and Zoopla are well-used online property portals that allow you to search for properties available for sale. If you're looking to flip a house, these platforms are a great way to search for properties that meet your investment criteria, such as location, price range, number of bedrooms and type and condition of the property.

They also offer a range of search filters that allow you to narrow down your search to properties that meet your specific criteria, such as location, price and property type. You can save your search preferences and set up alerts to receive notifications when new properties that match your criteria are listed.

Pros

- **Wide selection:** Rightmove and Zoopla have large databases of properties for sale, which can help you find a wide selection of properties to consider for flipping.

- **Search filters:** The search filters on these platforms allow you to narrow down your search based on specific criteria, such as location, price, number of bedrooms and more, making it easier to find properties that meet your needs.

- **Data and insights:** These platforms provide data and insights on property prices, such as how much similar properties on the same street are being sold for, bought for and when, as well as trends and demographics. This information can help you make informed decisions about which properties to flip and how to price them.

Cons

- **Competition:** Since Rightmove and Zoopla are popular platforms, there is a lot of competition for properties, which can drive up prices and make it harder to find good deals.

- **Inaccurate information:** The information on these platforms may not always be accurate or up to date, which can be frustrating and may lead you to waste time on properties that are no longer available or do not meet your needs. Estate agent photographs and layouts can also be misleading, as quite often the layouts are not to scale and photographs are taken to make the space appear bigger than in real life.

- **Limited property details:** While Rightmove and Zoopla provide basic property details, they may not provide all the information you need to make an informed decision about whether a property is worth flipping.

It's important to keep in mind that relying solely on these websites may not be the best way to find properties to flip. While they can be a great starting point, they may not have access to all the properties that are available for sale. Additionally, properties listed on these websites may already have multiple offers, which could drive up the purchase price and reduce your potential profit margin.

Estate agents

How they can work best for you

Using an estate agent can be a great way to access potential properties and make the buying process smoother. Building relationships with estate agents can provide numerous advantages for property developers, such as:

- **Access to off-market deals:** Estate agents often have access to properties that are not yet on the market or are being marketed discretely. Building a good relationship with an estate agent can give you an advantage in accessing these deals before they become widely available. One of the best ways to build great relationships with agents and get access to off-market properties, if possible, is to give them some of your existing rental properties to manage.

- **Knowledge of the local market:** Estate agents have an in-depth knowledge of the local property market, including property values, trends and demand. By building a relationship with an agent, you can tap into this expertise and gain valuable insights that can help you make informed decisions when buying or selling property.

- **Referrals and recommendations:** A good estate agent will have a network of contacts in the property industry, including other agents, investors and developers. By building a relationship with an agent, you can tap into this network and receive referrals and recommendations for other professionals who can help you with your property development projects.

- **Negotiating power:** When it comes to negotiating deals, having a good relationship with an estate agent can give you an advantage. Agents are often more willing to negotiate with developers they have a good relationship with, as they know that the developer is serious about making a purchase and is likely to be a repeat customer.

- **Assistance with property sales:** If you're selling your flipped property, having a good relationship with an estate agent can help you to get your properties seen by the right people. Estate agents have access to a wide range of buyers and can help you to market your properties effectively and achieve a quick and profitable sale.

Non-platform ways of property hunting

To increase your chances of finding the best property to flip, it's important to use a variety of methods for property hunting. Outlined below are some traditional pre-platform ways that still work and that many flippers I have worked with use frequently.

Local newspaper property adverts (they still work)

With online marketing portals dominating these days, this good old-fashioned way can often be overlooked by the masses. You can find some great opportunities with a lot less competition.

- **Local focus:** Many newspapers have a local focus, which can be beneficial when searching for properties in a specific area. This can help you to identify opportunities that may not be as visible on national or online platforms.

- **Direct negotiation opportunities:** When using newspaper ads, there may be more opportunities to negotiate with sellers directly, rather than through an estate agent. This can potentially result in a better deal on the property.

- **Beating the competition:** Because many buyers may focus their search online, using newspaper ads to find properties can reduce competition and increase the chances of finding a good deal.

- **Focus on renovation/repair:** Newspapers often advertise properties that are in need of renovation or repairs, which can present a great opportunity for investors to flip them and make a good profit.

Property developer networking events

Property developer network events can provide some great advantages when looking to find a property to buy and flip:

- **Gain insider information:** These events can give you access to insider information that can help you find the best property deals. By networking with developers and other industry professionals, you may be able to learn about off-market opportunities, upcoming development projects and emerging areas before they become public knowledge. Developers often have a hub of current listings that don't quite fit their needs, which can be a great way of finding properties not yet on the radar of others.

- **Grow your contact lists:** Attending property networking events is a great way of increasing your contacts in this area.

- **Meet potential partners:** These events can provide opportunities to meet potential partners, such as estate agents, contractors and investors, who can help you find and evaluate properties, provide funding for your flip and manage the renovation process.

- **Build relationships with other industry professionals:** By developing a reputation as a serious and reliable flipper, you may be able to establish a network to work with on future projects.

- **Learn from the best:** By meeting and learning from more experienced investors who have successfully flipped properties, you can gain valuable insights into the property market and develop a better understanding of the strategies and tactics that work best in your local market.

- **Keep up to date:** Property developer networking events can also provide opportunities to stay up to date with industry trends, regulations and changes in the local property market. By staying informed, you can make more educated decisions when evaluating potential properties and developing your investment strategy.

Ways to build your network

- **Search online for property developer networking events in your area:** Use keywords such as 'property developer networking events [your city]' and you should be able to make a list of upcoming events.

- **Check industry publications:** Check out magazines such as *Blue Bricks* (https://bluebricksmagazine.com) for listings of upcoming networking events. These types of publications often feature event calendars or directories.

- **Contact industry associations to inquire about upcoming events:** For example, the British Property Federation (https://bpf.org.uk) and WhiteBox Property Solutions (https://whiteboxps.com). often host networking events for their members.

- **Attend networking events at property developers' conferences:** You can find information about upcoming conferences on industry websites, such as The Property Investor Show (https://propertyinvestor.co.uk) or FutureBuild (https://futurebuild.co.uk), both of which have great events throughout the UK.

- **Follow property developer groups on social media platforms:** Look at LinkedIn, Facebook and Twitter. These groups often share information about upcoming events and opportunities to connect with other professionals in the industry.

Thinking outside the box when searching for a property to flip can open up new opportunities and potentially lead to greater profits. Traditional methods of property search, such as working with an estate agent or trawling online listings, can be limited and may not uncover all the available options. By exploring unconventional methods, such as networking with industry professionals, attending auctions or reaching out to distressed homeowners, you can find unique and potentially lucrative investment opportunities. This can also help you stand out in a competitive market to find properties that may not have been considered by others, giving you a greater advantage in your property flipping endeavours.

Contacting owners or landlords directly

Opportunity knocks (on doors)

If you have already narrowed down the area you want to buy in – or even the right street – but there isn't anything on the market, consider popping a note through letterboxes or, better still, knocking on doors and introducing yourself. Some people consider selling their house for years and by asking them the question, you might encourage them to take the plunge and sell to you. You never know, you could strike gold! By agreeing to make the sale privately, the seller will have the added bonus of not having to pay estate agents' fees. Top tips for door-to-door enquiries:

- **Go at the weekend:** You are more likely to catch people at home.

- **Be prepared for rejection:** Say you are moving into the area and like the street and ask if they know of anyone considering putting their house up for sale. (Only say this only if you plan to live there; neighbours may feel resentment when they realise you aren't moving in yourself.)

Be a detective

When you find properties that look run down and empty, contact the owners directly. These are some quick and easy steps you can take to find out who owns the property if you are unsure:

- **Check the HM Land Registry website:** If the property is registered, you should be able to find the owner's details here (https://gov.uk/government/organisations/land-registry).

- **Ask the neighbours:** If the property is not registered, try asking the neighbours or local authorities for information about the owner. They may have some knowledge about the owner or the property's history.

- **Use online platforms:** The online property portals mentioned earlier can help you find the owner of a property. As well as Zoopla and Rightmove, there's OnTheMarket (https://onthemarket.com).

- **Hire some help:** If you're still struggling to identify the owner, you may want to consider hiring a solicitor or property agent. They can help you track down the owner and assist you with the legal process of buying the property.

- **Place an ad:** If all else fails, consider placing an advert in the local newspaper. This may help you get in touch with someone who has knowledge of the property.

If the property is abandoned or has been left unoccupied for a long period of time, it may be subject to adverse possession laws. This means that someone else may be able to claim ownership of the property if they have occupied it for a certain period of time. It would be worth seeking legal advice before purchasing if this is the case.

Approach landlords with vacant properties

If these properties have been vacant for a while, the owner might well to be open to selling them, since they are costing money to run and aren't bringing them in any money by sitting empty. A keen buyer on the owner's doorstep can often be the answer to all their problems.

If the property appears habitable, I would suggest looking on online portals to see if you can find it under the 'for rent' section. The methods described above are also worth pursuing if you don't have any luck finding the landlord.

Ask friends and family to put the feelers out

My mum is the hub of all knowledge when it comes to what is going on in the local area. Her local knitting group can pin down three upcoming properties in one session. 'Jean's daughter has just landed a job in London and will need to relocate…', 'Steve and Jane have just split up and they will need to sell the house soon…' and so on.

The right property for the right area

Flipping a property successfully involves finding the right property in the right location, buying it at the right price and making the right renovations to maximise its value. But how do you find the right property in the right area?

It is always good to start by researching the property market in the area where you plan to flip. Look at recent sales data, property values and trends in the area to get an idea of which types of properties are in demand and what renovations or upgrades buyers are looking for. Consider the location of the property from where you are based – for your first few flips, properties in close proximity are ideal.

Determine how much you can afford to spend on a property and the renovations needed to flip it. This will help you to narrow down your search to properties that fit within your budget.

Once you've found a property that you're interested in, thoroughly inspect it to assess its condition. Look for any major repairs that will be needed and factor those into your renovation budget.

Look for properties in areas that are in high demand, with good schools, amenities and a strong job market. This will make it easier to sell the property once it has been renovated.

Consider the potential ROI for the property, taking into account the purchase price, renovation costs and estimated resale value. Aim for a property with a high potential ROI to maximise your profits.

Other potential magnets for buyers include:

- **Local transport networks:** Check out the local transport networks, which can have a huge impact on the end user. A good train or bus service into the nearest city can be a huge draw for commuters.

- **Local schools:** Ofsted reports are a great way of finding out if the local schools are good, which will largely attract families to the area.

- **Local amenities:** Check to see if there are any local supermarkets, shops, cafés, bars or even a local cinema. All factors to target your renovation towards as these will have an impact on your end user.

- **Local healthcare:** Check to see if there is a local GP surgery, dentist or even a hospital.

Good sources of information

Local environmental agencies can tell you if the property is located in a flood zone and what type of flood risk it may face. You can also find out if it is in or near protected areas or habitats for endangered species, which may affect the use and development of the property. Property prices, crime statistics and average earnings of an area can be found at https://zoopla.co.uk.

CASE STUDY: Think outside the box on location

In the post-pandemic world, it can pay to look beyond traditional methods of determining ceiling prices of properties.

Macclesfield is a medium-sized town, 20 miles south of Manchester. It dates back to medieval times, becoming an eighteenth-century boom town through the silk trade. Ten years ago, the town was quite run down, with high unemployment and a lot of derelict mills, which no longer had a purpose.

Positioned on the edge of the Peak District National Park and on the main line from London and Manchester, it now has a lot of appeal for former city dwellers with good disposable income now working from home.

In the past two years, house prices have increased by almost 50%. With the Peak District on the doorstep and good access into Manchester within twenty minutes (and London in 1 hour 40 minutes), it has meant that people can have the best of both worlds, which has had a positive impact on the value of properties in the area.[4]

---

4   A Greensmith, 'Average House Price in Macclesfield Up Almost Fifty Per Cent Since 2019', *Macclesfield News Hub* (29 January 2023), https://macclesfield.nub.news/property/property-of-the-week/average-house-price-in-macclesfield-up-almost-fifty-per-cent-since-2019, accessed 11 October 2023

How to recognise up-and-coming areas

Recognising up-and-coming areas can appear challenging. It may feel like having to look into a crystal ball. If you look a bit closer you will be able to find many indicators that an area may be up-and-coming. These include:

- **Increasing property values:** A significant increase in property values over a short period may indicate that an area is becoming more desirable.

- **New developments and construction:** The presence of new buildings, shops and businesses may indicate that an area is attracting investment and undergoing revitalisation.

- **Demographic changes:** Changes in demographics, such as an influx of younger professionals, may signal that an area is becoming more popular.

- **Transportation improvements:** The development of new subway or bus lines, for example, can increase accessibility and attract investment.

- **Cultural and recreational amenities:** An increase in new museums, parks or restaurants, for example, can make an area more attractive to residents and visitors.

- **Crime rates:** A decrease in crime can indicate that an area is becoming safer and more desirable.

- **Economic growth:** An increase in job opportunities can indicate that an area is becoming more prosperous.

- **Desirable shops moving into town:** Large chains such as John Lewis, M&S and Waitrose are all indicators that an area is worth investing in. Companies like these spend a lot of money researching areas before opening stores.

It is also worth contacting your local planning authority to see what is in the pipeline for the area and if there have been any recent government cash injections.

CASE STUDY: Research planning applications for amenities

One of the properties I sold recently increased in value by 30% without any renovation, simply because the mostly derelict row of shops five minutes' walk away from the property had been changed into good-quality wine bars and restaurants. There was also a new supermarket built within walking distance on what had been wasteland when I initially bought the property.

By investigating local planning applications before the purchase, I gained valuable insight into the local area and its visions for the future. This smart research paid dividends when it came to selling my property, increasing its value by 30% in just twelve months, without so much as opening a tin of paint. This particular property was on a quiet leafy road behind the bars and restaurants, so lack of noise pollution was an added bonus for the value increase.

This was bought as a buy and hold with tenant, however with the significant increase in value in such a short period of time, I decided to sell the property and invest the profit into other ventures.

Who is your property for?

You have done your research on the area; now it is time to find the right property to work best with the area you are looking to concentrate on. You must visit the area – have a good look around and see what and who is about.

Finding the right property to flip at the right price to make a tidy profit is one of the most difficult and time-consuming parts of the process, but time invested now will save you headaches and money later on. Getting it right is key to the success of your budding property flipping business and will make the process of selling with a good ROI so much easier further down the line. Common factors to keep in mind are closely linked to the section on ceiling prices in Chapter 3.

Different homeowners have different needs

- **Students:** Looking for affordable properties with good local amenities, transport and/or bike storage.

- **Families:** Wanting good schools, parking, healthcare, a garden and supermarkets nearby.

- **Business professionals:** Seeking good layout, finishes and attention to detail – they generally have no time to work on a property once moved in.

- **First-time buyers:** Happy with a cheaper property with a small garden and supermarkets nearby.

Due diligence

When you've identified a property to flip, you won't have had a full survey yet, but what you can find out now? The more information you gain early on will mean more value down the line and more profit in your pocket. Flipping a property can be a significant investment, and you need to ensure that it is a sound financial decision. Conducting due diligence now can help you assess the property's market value, determine any repair or renovation costs and estimate potential profits. You should also review any outstanding debts on the property that could affect your investment.

Doing your due diligence before you buy a property to flip is important for several reasons. Make sure you are aware of any potential issues as soon as a property is on your radar (if possible, even before it goes on the market or is listed at auction, so you can make a quick, informed decision). It can also help you identify any legal issues related to the property, such as zoning restrictions, building code violations or outstanding property taxes. Addressing these issues before purchasing the property can help you avoid potential legal problems and save you time and money in the long run.

Before purchasing a property to flip, it's important to research the local property market to understand the demand for properties in the area, the prices of comparable homes and any trends that could affect the property's value. This information can help you make informed decisions about the potential profitability of your investment.

Conducting due diligence can also help you plan for the renovation or repair process. You can identify any necessary permits, materials and labour costs and develop a realistic timeline for completing the project.

As the presenter of property refurbishment on behalf of the National Residential Landlords Association, Henry Davis has managed hundreds of developments over the last thirty years. He advises jumping on due diligence right away:

> 'You must complete your due diligence well before exchange of contracts. As soon as the deal has been agreed, I'm immediately on the phone to my quantity surveyor, my architect,

my solicitor, my planner and my structural engineer, if necessary, to arrange an immediate site visit. If I'm buying something from the auction, then I won't wait for the official auction house viewing. I will immediately visit that property and persuade whoever answers the door to give me a viewing. That way I've done all my due diligence and research long before the first official auction house viewing.'[5]

Evaluating the property

Take a structural engineer and quantity surveyor (QS) with you to the viewing.

Factors that can decrease the value of a property include:

- Japanese knotweed – an invasive plant species known for its aggressive growth and destructive impact on ecosystems and properties.

- If there is no planning consent for expansion or renovation. This can also be important if you are considering a change of use, for example from an office to an apartment.

- If the property is in a green belt area – typically, an undeveloped or sparsely developed region of land, often located on the outskirts of urban

---

5   H Davis, personal communication (2023)

areas. These areas are protected from extensive development to promote environmental conservation and maintain a balance between urban and rural spaces.

- If the property is in a conservation area with no allowance for development.

Henry Davis has more advice on this:

'You need to accurately scope out the project, get the specification tied down and accurately cost each part of the project so that there's no hidden extras suddenly appearing in the middle of a project. The only professional used by all the major housebuilders who can help you achieve this is your QS.'[6]

Find out if the property is listed by checking the National Heritage List for England (NHLE) (https://historicengland.org.uk/listing/the-list). The NHLE is the official database of all listed buildings in England. You can search for properties by postcode, street address or name, and the database includes information about the building's grade and listing status. Historic England is a public body that oversees the protection of England's historic environment. They also have a database that includes all listed buildings, scheduled monuments and registered parks and gardens in England.

---

6 H Davis, personal communication (2023)

If the property is listed, any alterations or renovations will require special permission from the local planning authority as there may be restrictions on what changes you can make to the building. Your local council will have a conservation officer who can also advise you on whether a property is listed or not. They may also be able to provide you with a copy of the listing details if the property is indeed listed.

Summary

- Finding the right investment property is crucial for achieving the highest ROI.

- Careful research, analysis and due diligence are necessary to identify properties with long-term value appreciation or high rental yields.

- Factors such as location, market demand, property condition and future development prospects should be considered when selecting an investment property.

- A well-chosen property with strong growth prospects can generate substantial capital gains.

- Properties with high rental demand can provide a steady stream of income.

- Thoroughly researching the investment property minimises risks associated with underperforming or low resale value properties.

- Efficient use of resources is ensured by making informed decisions during the property selection process.

- Assessing factors like property market trends, demographics and economic indicators helps in making the best possible ROI.

- Analysing comparable property sales and rental rates in the area provides insights into the property's potential financial performance.

- Engaging professionals such as real estate agents, property inspectors and financial advisers can aid in the decision-making process.

5
Securing The Deal

Now you know what you want, how do you get it?

Sealing the deal requires effective negotiation skills and a clear understanding of the buying process. This chapter will provide you with an in-depth exploration of the proven strategies and techniques that you can use to successfully close a deal when buying a property to flip.

We will examine the various factors that can impact the negotiation process, such as market conditions, the seller's motivations and the property's condition. Additionally, we will discuss the importance of high-level due diligence, including inspection, appraisal and title search, in ensuring that the deal is a sound investment. I will also provide practical tips on how to handle common challenges and objections that may arise during the negotiation process. By the end of this chapter, you will have a comprehensive understanding of how to effectively negotiate and seal the deal when buying a property to flip, setting you up for success in your property flipping journey.

Flipping a property can be an exciting and lucrative venture for many property investors. To successfully flip a property, you must have a solid understanding of the various financing options available. This chapter will provide an overview of the different ways in which you can finance a property flip, including traditional bank loans, hard money loans, bridging loans, private money loans and creative financing strategies. We will examine the benefits and drawbacks of each option, as well as the specific requirements and qualifications needed to obtain financing. You will gain a comprehensive understanding of the different financing options available to you, allowing you to make informed decisions when pursuing your next property flip.

Choosing the right method to raise money to buy a house to flip requires careful consideration. It requires a lot of knowledge and experience in property investing, as well as the ability to manage a renovation project. If you are attempting your first flip and don't have these skill sets, I have suggested below some ways to access the expertise you need.

Understanding your finances: A checklist

Before you try to buy, think about:

- **Your financial situation:** Consider how much money you have available for a down payment, as well as your credit score and debt-to-income ratio. This will help you determine which financing options you are eligible for.

- **The property's location:** Different areas may have different financing options available.

- **The property's value:** The purchase price and resale value. This will help you determine how much money you need to borrow and how much profit you can expect to make.

- **The timeline for the project:** Some financing options, such as bridging loans, may have shorter repayment periods and higher interest rates.

- **Your experience level:** Consider your ability to manage the project and handle unexpected expenses. Some financing options, such as joint venture partnerships, may provide additional support and expertise that can help mitigate risks.

- **Cost of financing:** Think about the interest rates, fees and terms of each financing option. Calculate the total cost of financing for each option to determine which is the most cost-effective.

Disclaimer: I am not a professional in the financial aspects of property investing. The methods above are highlighting possible ways to help fund your flip. Before you take on any of the investments mentioned here, it is always worth seeking financial advice from a professional, who will be able to highlight the implications and professional practices with any route you decide is best for you.

Raising the finances with zero funds

Buying an investment property with zero funds in the bank may seem like a challenging endeavour, but rest assured it can be done. With the right strategies, networking and creative financing, it is possible to embark on the path to property ownership and start successfully building wealth through real estate investments.

Remortgaging on your existing property

This can be a beneficial way to secure finance for a property flip as it allows you to tap into the equity you have built up in your current property. If your property has appreciated in value since you purchased it or if you have paid down a significant portion of your mortgage, remortgaging can provide you with access to a substantial amount of capital. This capital can then be used as a down payment or to finance the entire purchase of the property you intend to flip.

Remortgaging can often offer lower interest rates compared to other forms of borrowing, such as personal loans or credit cards. By leveraging the equity in your existing property, you can take advantage of these lower rates and potentially save money on interest payments over the course of your property flip project.

It also provides flexibility in terms of repayment. Depending on the terms of your new mortgage, you may have the option to extend the repayment period, which can result in lower monthly payments. This can be particularly helpful during the renovation and sale process, as it gives you more financial breathing room.

Lastly, remortgaging your existing property allows you to retain ownership and control over your home while still accessing the funds needed for your property flip. This means you can continue living in your current property and potentially benefit from any future appreciation in its value.

Mortgages

If you need a mortgage, having a mortgage in principle in place before viewing a property on the market is crucial. Knowing how much you can borrow will give you a clear idea of your budget, save you time and prevent disappointment. A pre-approved mortgage will also demonstrate to sellers that you are a serious buyer, which can give you an advantage in a competitive housing market

Friends and family

It's common to have family and friends partner up on a property flip (potentially with a combination of some partners needing a mortgage and some contributing cash).

Partnering with friends and family can provide several benefits, such as pooling resources, sharing responsibilities and having a support system. You may be more comfortable working with people you know and trust. Moreover, if everyone involved has a clear understanding of the roles and responsibilities and is committed to working together, it can be a successful partnership.

If this is your chosen method, it's important to ensure that everyone involved is on the same page regarding financial goals, timelines and risk tolerance. Disagreements over these issues can strain personal relationships and lead to costly mistakes. Moreover, even with a good plan in place, there is always the potential for unforeseen problems to arise, such as unexpected repair costs, delays in the renovation process or difficulty finding a buyer.

My advice would be to have a written legal agreement drawn up outlining everyone's responsibilities and expectations. It's crucial to keep everything well documented so you have a paper trail that any partner may consult if questions arise later. It's important to have honest and open communication with potential partners, to carefully consider the risks and rewards, and to have a solid plan in place before making any decisions.

A business partner

Starting a house flipping business with a business partner can have its own unique set of advantages and disadvantages.

The positives include access to double the finances, skills and expertise, while splitting the workload and responsibilities:

- **Shared financial resources:** With a business partner, you can pool your financial resources and invest in more properties than you could on your own.
- **Shared skills and expertise:** Your partner may have skills or expertise that complement yours, such as construction knowledge, design skills or project management experience.
- **Shared workload:** You can split the workload and responsibilities, which can be especially helpful if you both have full-time jobs or other commitments.

On the negative side, you will be splitting the profits and there are many potential areas for conflict:

- **Shared profits:** When you have a partner, you will have to split the profits from the house flipping business, which could impact your financial goals. It's worth noting that the need to share details of all your personal finances with your partner may not be to everyone's liking!

- **Conflict:** With a partner, there is always the potential for conflicts to arise, whether it's over financial decisions, project management or creative differences.

Before starting a business with a partner, make sure you are both on the same page from the outset with a legal document in place that outlines each person's responsibilities, ownership percentage and how profits will be split. This can help smooth out the process should conflicts arise further down the line.

If you have complementary skills and trust each other, a partnership could be a great way to grow your business. If you have different goals or have difficulty working collaboratively, it may be better to start the business with another financial set-up.

Types of mortgages

Bridging loan

A bridging loan is a type of short-term financing that is used to bridge a gap between two larger and more permanent financing solutions. They are typically used to provide temporary financing for a property purchase, while waiting for longer-term financing to become available. They are commonly used in property transactions when a buyer needs to purchase a new property before their existing property is sold or when a property is being purchased at auction and a quick turnaround is required.

A bridging loan could be used in the auction purchase of an off-market below-market-value purchase. It could just help with the purchase cost or it may provide finance for the refurbishment works, depending on the projected end value and the amount required. Bridging or refurbishment/development loans can be flexible and used either for speed or to refurbish otherwise uninhabitable properties.

When choosing a good bridging loan company, Roma Finance have a useful bridging guide for beginners, which may help give you an insight into what is available.[7]

Buy-to-let loan

A buy-to-let loan is a type of mortgage loan specifically designed for people who want to buy a property with the intention of renting it out to tenants.

---

7   S Williamson, 'A Beginner's Guide to Bridging & Development Lending', *Property Reporter* (6 March 2023), https://propertyreporter.co.uk/academy/a-beginners-guide-to-bridging-development-lending, accessed 12 October 2023

The loan is typically secured against the property being purchased, and the lender will take into account the potential rental income that the property could generate when assessing the borrower's ability to repay the loan. Buy-to-let loans usually require a larger deposit than traditional residential mortgages and often have higher interest rates, as they are considered riskier investments by lenders due to the potential for fluctuating rental incomes and property values. They can be a great product to help enable individuals to invest in property with the goal of generating rental income and potential long-term capital growth.

Samantha Williamson from Roma Finance notes:

> 'A popular strategy now is serviced accommodation (SA) or holiday lets. They may also fall under the buy-to-let (BTL) definition, but be careful as not all lenders have that product available. You are best to speak to a whole-of-market mortgage broker with experience of BTL and commercial mortgages.
>
> 'Be careful in the current market as base rate increases over a relatively short period of time have meant that some BTL loans are much lower than previously due to how the lenders calculate their stressed rental cover tests. If you have a high capital value property in an area that's generally for owner occupiers, the likelihood is that you won't be able to get a

75% loan to value (LTV) mortgage – it will be lower.'[8]

How to deal with a volatile interest rate climate

With interest rates continually fluctuating, be prepared by incorporating variable rates into your financial planning and stress-testing your budget to ensure you can handle higher interest rates if they occur. It's also essential to maintain a long-term perspective. Property markets are cyclical and interest rates can fluctuate over time. Focus on building a sustainable financial plan that can withstand market ups and downs.

Buy-to-develop grants

There are several grants available in the UK to support buying a property to develop into a house, which can come in handy if you are flipping an old house. These include:

- **Renovation loan:** This is a loan provided by the government to help homeowners make improvements or repairs to their homes. The maximum loan amount is £25,000 and the interest rate is fixed for the duration of the loan.
- **The Clean Heat Grant:** This scheme provides vouchers worth up to £4,000 to help homeowners

---

[8] S Williamson, personal communication (2023)

make energy-efficient improvements to their homes. The grant goes towards the cost of a new renewable heating system.

- **Community Housing Fund:** This grant is available to community-led groups that want to build affordable homes for rent or sale in their local area. The grant offers up to £4 million in funding for projects that meet certain eligibility criteria.

It's important to note that grant availability and eligibility can change, so it's always best to check the latest information from the relevant government department or local authority (www.gov.uk is a great source of information for all current government grants available).

Understanding chains

The process of buying a property typically involves several steps, which are often referred to as 'chains' in the property industry. A property chain refers to a sequence of buyers and sellers who are linked because they are buying and selling properties from each other.

Here are the typical steps in a property chain:

1. **Finding a property:** The first step is to find a suitable property that meets your needs and budget. You can do this by browsing property listings online or through estate agents.

2. **Making an offer:** Once you find a property you are interested in, you will need to make an offer to the seller. The seller may accept your offer or negotiate a different price.

3. **Conveyancing:** After your offer is accepted, you will need to hire a conveyancer or solicitor to handle the legal aspects of the transaction. This includes conducting searches, reviewing contracts and transferring ownership.

4. **Survey and mortgage:** You may need to get a survey done on the property to identify any potential issues or repairs that need to be made. You will also need to secure a mortgage from a lender.

5. **Exchange of contracts:** Once all the legal and financial aspects are in place, you and the seller will sign a contract and exchange it. This legally binds both parties to the sale.

6. **Completion:** On the completion date, the sale is finalised and the money is transferred to the seller. You can then take possession of the property and move in.

It's important to note that delays or issues at any stage of the property chain can cause problems for all parties involved. For example, if one sale falls through, it can affect everyone in the chain. This can often become a frustrating situation for all parties as it can prolong the time frame of your flip – sometimes by weeks.

Here are some steps that you can take to handle the situation:

- **Be in the know:** Find out the reason why the chain has broken and how it may affect your purchase. Speak to your estate agent, solicitor or conveyancer to get a clear understanding of the situation.

- **Weigh up your options:** Depending on the circumstances, you may have a few options available to you. You could wait for the chain to be fixed, look for a different property or negotiate a new deal with the seller.

- **Keep your solicitor informed:** Tell them about the situation and any decisions you make. They can advise you on the legal implications of any actions you take and help you navigate the process.

- **Talk to the seller:** It's important to maintain good communication with the seller, especially if you're considering renegotiating the deal. Try to be understanding of their situation and work together to find a solution.

- **Be patient:** If the chain has broken, it's likely that there will be delays. Be patient, but don't be afraid to ask for regular updates from your solicitor or estate agent.

- **Consider a loan:** If you're in a hurry to complete the purchase, you may want to consider getting a bridging loan (see above).

Tax implications (capital gains)

When it comes to selling your flip it is important to take capital gains tax (CGT) into consideration, which may be incurred within your budget. This is a tax you may have to pay when you sell an asset that has increased in value. This includes selling a house that is not your primary residence, such as a second home or a buy-to-let property.

When you sell a property that is subject to CGT, you will need to calculate the gain you have made by subtracting the purchase price, plus any costs of buying and selling the property, from the sale price. You will then need to pay CGT on this gain at the applicable rate, which varies depending on your income and the amount of the gain. It is paramount that you keep your receipts for all your purchases to submit to your accountant.

If the property you're selling is your primary residence, you may be eligible for private residence relief, which means that you won't have to pay CGT on any gain you make when you sell your home. If you have lived in the property for only part of the time you owned it, or have used it for business purposes, the amount of relief you can claim may be reduced. These factors can help you decide whether you live in your flip while renovating (depending on if it is habitable) or having your flip as a second property.

Stamp duty

Stamp Duty Land Tax (SDLT) is a tax that is levied on the purchase of property. It applies to both freehold and leasehold properties, as well as to property transfers that are made as gifts. The amount of stamp duty tax that is payable depends on the value of the property being purchased and the circumstances of the buyer.

In England and Northern Ireland, the SDLT rates for residential property purchases are currently:

- **Up to £125,000:** 0%
- **£125,001–£250,000:** 2%
- **£250,001–£925,000:** 5%

Different rules apply for first-time buyers and those purchasing additional properties, such as buy-to-let investments, so it is worth investigating these if you fall into these categories. In Scotland and Wales, different tax systems apply. You can access a stamp duty calculator on the government website.[9]

---

9   GOV.UK, 'Calculate Stamp Duty Land Tax (SDLT)', https://tax.service.gov.uk/calculate-stamp-duty-land-tax, accessed 12 October 2023

The sales process

You have done all your research, found the perfect property to flip and it's the time to buy. This is where the fun begins! We've covered how platforms and estate agents work above, but here are some other ways you can buy.

Private purchase (direct with seller)

If you find a property through contact with the seller directly, you can purchase the property directly with them without an estate agent. This may be a more cost-effective method, but there are drawbacks, such as managing the process as outlined above yourself, including negotiating the purchase price. This can be time consuming and sometimes frustrating, and you will probably have to do a lot of chasing.

If negotiating yourself, be realistic on your offers. Offering too low may lead to blowing yourself out of the water at first base. Equally, it is important to hold your nerve. Some of the savviest developers I have worked with have walked away from counter offers that don't fit their budget, sometimes leading to the seller coming back to them with a better offer if they are desperate to sell. You may need to negotiate on other terms, such as the completion date, as well as price.

You will still need a solicitor or conveyancer to handle the legal aspects of the purchase, such as checking the title, conducting searches and handling the transfer of funds. Once all the necessary checks have been carried out and the mortgage has been approved, you can exchange contracts with the seller and complete the sale. You will then become the legal owner of the property.

Auctions

As discussed earlier, before the auction you need to do your research on the properties being auctioned and decide which ones you are interested in bidding for. You should also arrange for a survey and legal checks to be carried out on any properties you are considering.

Roma Finance offers a great service for auction buyers called the RomaFLOW process, available to its light refurbishment range.[10] Their fast-bridging channel allows buyers to complete in twenty-eight days and they can provide an agreement in principle in advance of an auction so you have certainty and a ceiling price, giving you the chance to bid confidently.

The auction process runs as follows:

---

10 Roma, 'Roma Finance launches fast new processing channel – #RomaFLOW', https://romafinance.co.uk/the-hub/roma-finance-launches-fast-new-processing-channel-romaflow, accessed 12 October 2023

SECURING THE DEAL

1. **Registration:** On the day of the auction, you will need to register as a bidder and provide proof of identity and payment details.

2. **Bidding:** Once the auction starts, bidding will begin on the properties you are interested in. It's important to set a maximum bid limit and stick to it.

3. **Winning bid:** If you are the winning bidder, you will be required to pay a deposit (usually 10% of the purchase price) and sign a contract on the day of the auction.

4. **Completion:** The completion date is usually set for twenty-eight days after the auction. On completion day, you will need to pay the remaining balance of the purchase price and any associated fees.

When buying a property at auction, you will be entering into a legally binding contract as soon as the hammer falls, so it's crucial to do your due diligence beforehand and seek professional advice if necessary.

In all these scenarios it's important to resist temptation to go above your profit margin, especially in an auction. All too often your emotional attachment will start creeping in. Remember this is now a business and not a hobby, and staying within your budget at this stage will affect how much profit you will make when it comes to selling the property once flipped.

Belt and braces: What survey do you need?

There are several types of surveys you can have that can help you identify any potential problems with the property at various levels, estimate its value and ensure that you are making a sound investment. All come at different cost levels, but it may be worth the investment in the long run to carry out a more comprehensive report. The different types of survey include:

- **Condition report/home survey:** This is the most basic type of survey, which is usually required by the mortgage lender to estimate the value of the property. The surveyor will visit the property and assess its condition, location and other factors to determine its worth.

- **Homebuyer report:** This is a more detailed survey that provides a comprehensive assessment of the property's condition. The surveyor will inspect the property and report any defects, including damp, structural issues and other potential problems.

- **Building survey:** This is the most comprehensive survey available and is recommended for older properties or those that have undergone significant alterations. The surveyor will inspect the property in detail and provide a comprehensive report on its condition, including advice on any repairs that may be required.

While a survey can provide valuable information, it cannot identify all potential issues with a property. It is also important to choose a reputable surveyor who is a member of a professional body, such as the Royal Institution of Chartered Surveyors (RICS).

Many developers who I work with recommend having a more comprehensive survey, which helps to seal due diligence at the final stage with a belt-and-braces approach. This can often help in leveraging a negotiation on price due to work needing to be carried out.

The final hurdles: How to make time move faster

Make positive use of the inevitable delays as you wait for your purchase to complete. What can you get done so that you are ready to move quickly once you have acquired the property?

- Start to look at materials needed for the job.
- Check out potential contractors and professionals needed to make the job run as smoothly as possible, such as an architect, structural engineer and interior designer. This is also a good

time to start looking at specific contractors. Recommendations are a good way to ensure the contractor is reliable and will carry out the job to the expected level.

- Study your renovation plan, including critical dates you need to achieve.

Summary

- Develop a good understanding of your local property market and the demand for the type of property you are considering.

- Research and analyse market trends, property sales data and rental rates to gauge demand and potential profitability.

- Build a team of reliable contractors and professionals, such as architects, interior designers and tradespeople, who can execute the renovation plan effectively.

- Create a detailed renovation plan that outlines the scope of work, budget and timeline for the project.

- Ensure access to financing options, whether through personal funds, loans or partnerships, to cover the purchase and renovation costs.

- Having all these components in place before purchasing a property increases the likelihood of completing the renovation on time and within budget.

- Thoroughly assess the property's condition and potential for improvement to determine its viability as a profitable project.

- Consider factors such as location, property size, existing infrastructure and potential for value appreciation during the renovation.

- Regularly communicate and coordinate with your team of contractors and professionals to ensure smooth project execution.

- Regularly review and track the progress of the renovation to stay on schedule and address any issues promptly.

- By completing the renovation on time and within budget, you increase your chances of selling the property for a profit.

In the next section we will discuss in depth how to manage a successful renovation and refurbishment project. This will include setting a realistic budget, scheduling necessary repairs and upgrades, and establishing a timeline for completion.

PART TWO
GETTING IT RIGHT

6
Managing Your Project

Managing the construction process and finishing touches when undertaking a flipping project on site can be a challenging but exciting task. Whether you're a seasoned property investor or a first-time flipper, knowing how to effectively manage the on-site work can either make or break your project. In this section, I will guide you through the essential steps of managing a flipping project on site, from creating a project plan and managing contractors to ensuring quality control, staying within budget and making the project work seamlessly.

Even if you've hired a quantity surveyor (QS) or a project manager (PM) (see below) you have to know how to manage them. Being fully prepared to brief them will save you time and headaches later.

Later in this section, I will also tell you how to get the maximum profit on your property flip and give you clarity and confidence on how to maximise the pre-market presentation of your property before listing.

Who is on your team?

Here's a closer look at the professionals who can help you through the design and construction process.

Project manager

Flipping a property often involves managing multiple tasks and coordinating various stakeholders, including architects, engineers, contractors and suppliers. A good PM has experience in managing a construction project from start to finish, efficiently, safely and on budget. They will be your day-to-day presence on site, ensuring everything runs as smoothly as possible, identifying potential problems early on, finding solutions before they become more expensive to fix, and identifying and mitigating risks. They can liaise with contractors, suppliers and stakeholders on your behalf, keep you informed about progress and ensure that everyone is on the same page.

Quantity surveyor

If you haven't hired a QS, I would recommend you do this, for several reasons. A QS will drive the

MANAGING YOUR PROJECT

budget, helping you identify and mitigate risks by providing accurate cost estimates and monitoring the project closely, ensuring your budget is apportioned most effectively.

A QS can provide ongoing cost management throughout the project, tracking expenses and providing regular updates on the project's financial status. This can help you make informed decisions about any changes or modifications to the project, ensuring that you remain within budget. They can help you negotiate contracts with contractors and subcontractors, ensuring that you get the best possible prices and terms. They can also review contracts to ensure that they are fair and protect your interests.

A QS can also act as a project manager, overseeing the entire process and ensuring that everything runs smoothly. They can help you find ways to save money without sacrificing quality. This process, known as value engineering, involves analysing the project to identify areas where costs can be reduced without compromising performance or functionality.

Hiring a quantity surveyor can help you save time, money and headaches during the property flipping process and ensure that your project is completed on time, within budget and to the highest standards of quality. They can advise on the most cost-effective construction methods and materials, while still meeting your desired outcome. This can be particularly important when working to a tight budget, as it can help keep costs down while still achieving your desired results.

As Henry Davis summarises:

> 'It's all about getting the right quantity surveyor. They will cost out the project in detail and will advise you on the best materials. They will cost out all materials via their bill of quantities and also help you with the scope of the project so there's no hidden extras. They will help you to tie down the specification and they will arrange the JCT [Joint Contracts Tribunal] contract, plus tender out any work between you and your builder. So, the quantity surveyor will reduce risks, professionalise the project and protect you from cowboy builders.'[11]

Structural engineer (for extensive renovations to pass building controls)

Flipping a property often involves renovating or remodelling, which may require changes to the building's structure. A structural engineer can assess the building's current structural integrity and identify any issues that need to be addressed before starting the work. They can ensure that the building is

---

11 H Davis, personal communication (2023)

structurally sound and that any changes to the structure will not compromise safety.

A structural engineer can help you ensure that your property flipping project is safe, complies with local building codes and regulations, and is cost-effective. They ensure that your project stays within budget and any structural changes are improving the value of the property. For example, they can suggest ways to increase the property's usable space, add structural features that are popular with buyers or make the building more energy efficient.

Architect

Hiring an architect can be a good investment that can help you achieve your goals and maximise your profits.

Architects are trained to design and plan buildings, and are experts at creating functional, aesthetically pleasing spaces. They can help you assess the potential of a property and create a cohesive design vision that maximises its value, working with you to determine which features are most important for your target market and helping you achieve a look and feel that will attract buyers.

Architects are knowledgeable about building codes and regulations, which means they can ensure that your renovations are up to code and that you won't run into any issues with permits or inspections.

They can help you manage your budget by creating a design that is cost-effective and avoids expensive mistakes. They can also help you prioritise your renovations and suggest alternative solutions to keep costs under control.

A well-designed and renovated property can command a higher price on the market. An architect can help you create a design that adds value to your property and makes it more attractive to potential buyers.

Planning permission and building regulations

Building regulations and planning permission set standards for construction work and cover things like structural safety, energy efficiency and fire safety. Planning permission is required for certain types of building work, such as significant alterations to the property's exterior or adding an extension.

When you need permission and how to apply

You will likely need to obtain both building regulations approval and planning permission, depending on the scope of the renovations you are undertaking. The best way to apply for these approvals is to contact your local authority's planning department, who will be able to guide you through the process and provide you with the necessary forms and information.

Failing to obtain the required approvals can lead to legal problems and may even prevent you from being able to sell the property in the future.

Listed building consent

Listed building consent is required when you plan to make changes to a listed building that may affect its historical or architectural significance. This consent is necessary even if you only plan to carry out minor alterations or repairs. Listed building consent applications are usually made to the local authority's planning department, and they will assess whether the proposed changes will preserve or enhance the building's historic character.

It is essential to check whether your property is listed, as failing to obtain the necessary consent can lead to penalties, fines or even legal action.

Extra units or extensions

If your property has a self-contained unit, consider turning this into a studio flat that can be rented out for additional side income or used for housing a family member, such as a granny, or a son or daughter who has chosen to live at home for a while longer.

This can be a valuable asset. Renting out the flat can generate additional income, which can help offset the property's mortgage payments and increase the property's overall value. This addition can appeal to potential buyers who are looking for a property with additional income-generating or family-friendly features.

CASE STUDY: Be prepared to pivot for success

We recently were asked to stage for sale a property in a village in Derbyshire that had been sitting on the market empty with no furniture or furnishings for seven months. The main house was a spacious three-bedroom property, suited to a family with teenagers, with the village having a good transport network to nearby Derby and Nottingham. The property also featured a detached, self-contained annex in the back garden, ideal for accommodating an elderly relative or serving as an extra private area, should any of the teenagers opt to reside at home for an extended period. We staged this space with this target demographic audience in mind and within a week of going back on the market, the property sold for 7% above the asking price.

If there is space to extend a property, it can be a good idea to get planning permission for a potential extension, even if the budget does not allow for the actual extension at the time of flipping. Having planning permission can add significant value to the property, making it more attractive to potential buyers who are looking for a property with the potential for expansion and most of the hard lifting already done and agreed. This option can also attract buyers who may be willing to take on the project themselves in the future, leading to a potentially higher selling price.

Additionally, obtaining planning permission early can save time and money if the new owner decides to carry out the extension in the future. This can also make the property stand out from other listings, increasing its overall value and contributing to a higher ROI for you.

The flow

Maximising the space and flow of the house can also make your property more attractive to potential buyers. One way to achieve this is by opening up the floor plan and creating an open living space. This can be done by either removing existing walls or expanding doorways between rooms to create a sense of continuity and flow.

Using neutral colours in all the rooms, as discussed in Chapter 2, can help make the space feel more spacious and airy and create a connection between the rooms, making the house feel connected as a whole. Later, other important aspects to consider are the placement of furniture and the use of standalone lighting to make the space feel more open and welcoming.

Multifunctional rooms

Creating a spare room as a flexible multifunctional space can also add significant value to a property. By making a spare room versatile, it can serve various purposes (such as a home office, guest bedroom or workout area), appeal to a broader range of potential buyers and make the property stand out from other listings.

The design process

The first step of the design process is to prepare drawings, which you will need to apply for planning permission and also to provide to the contractors you are inviting to tender for the work. Providing a comprehensive and accurate set of drawings and specifications to contractors is essential for ensuring that the project is completed to your satisfaction within budget and on time. The specific drawings required will depend on the scope of the project and the work that needs to be done.

Some common types of drawings that you may need to provide include floor plans, elevations and detailed specifications:

- **Floor plans to scale, including critical dimensions:** These are essential in showing the layout of the house, including the placement of walls, doors, windows and other fixtures. These drawings will help contractors understand the scope of the project and make accurate estimates of the materials and labour needed.

- **Electrical/M&E (by the M&E contractor):** Showing the electrical and mechanical positions and lighting layout. An M&E (mechanical and electrical) contractor specialises in the installation, maintenance and management of mechanical and electrical systems within buildings and infrastructure projects. They play a crucial role in ensuring that heating, ventilation, air-conditioning, electrical and other related systems operate efficiently and safely.

- **Elevations:** This is another critical set of drawings that show the exterior of the house, including the height, shape and materials used. These drawings are crucial for providing a clear picture of the desired finished product. They can help contractors understand the aesthetic and structural requirements of the project.

- **Fixed joinery drawings:** For items such as a built-in window seat, bespoke wardrobes or storage in an awkward or unusual space, or built-in cupboards or shelving. Having these drawings in place can clearly articulate what you are wanting to a joiner and save you a lot of time in the long run.

- **Detailed specifications:** These important documents should accompany the drawings. These specifications should detail the specific materials and finishes that are required, including any unique features or customisation that needs to be done. They should also outline any specific requirements related to quality, performance and sustainability.

It's likely that you will need to employ professionals to produce an accurate set of drawings. The main ones to use are:

- **An architect:** They can provide a complete set of drawings that include floor plans, elevations and detailed specifications. They can also provide design input and advice on the layout and functionality of the house.

- **A structural engineer:** They can provide drawings and calculations for any structural modifications or changes that need to be made to the house. They can also advise on any building code or permit requirements.

- **An interior designer:** They can provide drawings and specifications for any interior changes, including finishes, fixtures and furnishings. They can also provide design input and advice on creating a cohesive and appealing aesthetic.

MANAGING YOUR PROJECT

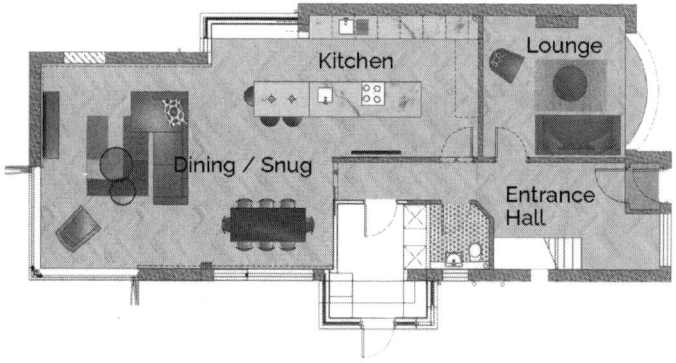

Ground floor layout – private residence, Didsbury, Manchester

How to incorporate sustainability into your project without breaking the bank

Incorporating sustainable design and construction practices into property flipping can not only benefit the environment but can actually save you money and enhance the property's appeal to environmentally conscious buyers. Here are some ideas you can adopt for sustainable practices:

- **Install energy-efficient appliances:** Choose ENERGY STAR-rated refrigerators, dishwashers, and heating, ventilation and air-conditioning (HVAC) systems to reduce energy consumption and appeal to eco-conscious buyers.

- **Solar panels:** Consider installing these to harness renewable energy and potentially reduce long-term energy costs for future occupants.

- **Eco-friendly building materials:** Opt for reclaimed wood, bamboo flooring, low VOC paints and recycled tiles to reduce the environmental impact of the renovation.

- **Energy-efficient windows:** Replace old windows with energy-efficient models to improve insulation and reduce heating and cooling demands.

- **Water conservation:** Install low-flow faucets, showerheads and dual-flush toilets to promote water conservation and reduce utility bills.

- **Improve the property's insulation:** This will enhance energy efficiency and comfort while minimising heating and cooling needs.

- **Landscape with native plants:** Use native and drought-resistant plants for landscaping, reducing water consumption and maintenance requirements.

- **Salvage and repurpose materials from the original structure:** Do this whenever possible to reduce waste and lower renovation costs.

- **Use energy-efficient LED bulbs:** Replace any traditional light bulbs to lower electricity consumption.

- **Use durable, high-quality materials:** These will stand the test of time, reducing the need for frequent replacements.

By integrating these sustainable design and construction practices into your property flip, you can make a positive impact on the environment while attracting a growing market of environmentally conscious buyers.

Finding reputable tradespeople

Finding reputable tradespeople can involve a significant investment of time and effort, as any delays or mistakes caused by 'cowboy subbies' can result in significant financial losses.

Working with reputable tradespeople means that you can trust that the work will be done correctly and to code. This is important not only for the safety and structural integrity of the house but also for any future buyers who will expect a well-built and safe home. Poor-quality work or shortcuts taken during the renovation process can result in serious problems down the line, such as leaks, electrical issues or even structural damage.

Experienced, reputable tradespeople will provide accurate estimates and avoid unexpected expenses, helping you stay within budget. They can offer valuable advice on materials, design and construction techniques that can save you money without sacrificing quality.

Here are some steps you can take to find reliable tradespeople:

- **Word of mouth:** Reach out to friends, family and acquaintances who have completed similar projects and ask for their recommendations. Word-of-mouth referrals are often the most reliable way to find good tradespeople.

- **Search online directories:** Use Yelp (https://yelp.co.uk) or Google Reviews (https://business.google.com/reviews) to find tradespeople who have a high number of positive reviews and a good overall rating.

- **Check licensing:** Ensure that the people you're considering are licensed and insured. Check this with the relevant licensing board or search online databases.

Tips on getting the right tradespeople include:

- **Making sure they are available when you need them:** Tradespeople can have a habit of disappearing halfway through the job and putting the project in jeopardy.

- **Block book:** Ensure you block book their time to prevent them getting tempted to jump on to another job.

- **Look at their supply chain:** Ask if they have stockpiles of materials and how long their lead is on certain items.

Managing payment of contractors

Another point to address when interviewing contractors is to check that they are willing to work with a Joint Contracts Tribunal (JCT) contract. This is a standard form contract, widely used in the construction industry, that sets out the terms and conditions governing the relationship between the employer (the person or organisation commissioning the work) and the contractor (the person or organisation carrying out the work).

They typically include clauses covering issues such as payment, variations, delays, insurance and dispute resolution. The aim is to provide a clear and fair framework for the parties involved in the construction project, and to ensure that the work is completed on time, on budget and to the required standard. If you are not using a JCT you will need an otherwise legally binding contract.

It's worth noting that a contract protects both parties – you (the developer) and the contractor – should you change the scope of the project while on site.

As Henry Davis says:

> 'On larger projects with multiple invoices, builders tend to front load the first two or three invoices. They then have a cash flow problem, and when this happens you are effectively paying for work that hasn't been done,

which effectively means you're paying in advance. The only way to stop this happening is by getting your quantity surveyor to independently verify the value of each invoice. That way you're not paying in advance, and you can control the money.

'The only way to control and manage a builder is by paying in arrears. Ideally up to four weeks, but even if it's as short as a week. You also need to get a JCT contract or at least have something in writing if it's a smaller project.'[12]

EMPLOYING YOUR WORKFORCE

Essential professionals to employ

- Architect
- Structural engineer

Non-essential professionals to consider

- Interior designer
- Electrical
- Plumber
- Joiner
- Decorator
- Tile fitter
- Flooring specialist

---

12 H Davis, personal communication (2023)

Set yourself up for success

In every job, problems and delays will arise. It's a part of the process, no matter how detailed and thorough you are in the planning stage. Suppliers will be late, contractors get behind and weather can put certain jobs on hold. Being able to make a positive use of these interruptions to your schedule can mean the difference in getting the job finished on time and on budget so you can release capital and move on to the next, rather than being late to complete with all the associated costs.

By following these tips, you can speed up the project timeline and increase your chances of completing on time and within budget:

- **Develop a detailed project plan:** This can help you stay organised and focused on completing the project on time. Break down the project into smaller tasks and assign realistic timelines to each task.

- **Hire experienced contractors:** These people can complete the work more efficiently and effectively, saving you time and money in the long run. Be sure to thoroughly vet any contractors you hire and check their references.

- **Order materials in advance:** This can help you avoid delays in the construction process. Make a list of all the materials you will need and order them as early as possible.

- **Factor in European shutdown of factories:** When considering suppliers, it's important to note that most European suppliers close their factories in August for routine machine maintenance and holidays. This can sometimes cause a delay on items such as ceramic tiles, carpets and light fittings. Having this knowledge in advance can help you prioritise ordering such items, avoiding potential delays.

- **Prioritise critical tasks:** Identify the critical tasks that need to be completed before others and prioritise them. This will help you avoid delays caused by unexpected issues or complications.

- **Set clear deadlines:** It's a good idea to do this for each task and hold yourself and your team accountable for meeting them. Regularly review progress against the project plan and adjust timelines as necessary.

- **Minimise change orders:** Finalise the scope of work before construction begins as change orders can add time and cost to the project.

- **Be flexible:** Unexpected issues and complications can arise during any construction project. Be prepared to adjust your timeline and plans as necessary to keep the project on track.

Foster community unity

Informing neighbours about your property flip can create a ripple effect of positivity within the surrounding community. By establishing transparent communication, you foster trust and goodwill among residents, demonstrating respect for their environment. This approach opens channels for dialogue, addressing any concerns early on and potentially garnering support for your project.

As neighbours witness the transformation taking place, a sense of shared excitement and involvement can flourish, instilling a stronger community spirit. The resulting harmony and collaboration contribute to a vibrant neighbourhood atmosphere, where everyone feels connected and invested in the progress, ultimately enhancing the overall quality of life for residents.

Shortlist the right tradespeople and contractors

A good time to research tradespeople and suppliers is while your property is going through the legal presale process, when you have your project clearly in mind but it has not started yet. You can then hit the ground running once the sale is completed.

Researching suppliers and labour ahead of the start can help you find the best deals on materials and ensure that you have everything you need before you start your project. This can save you time and money in the long run and ensure that your project stays within budget.

Because many of the good tradespeople are incredibly busy, you may wish to invite them on site to see the project. This helps with 'buy in' to your project and you can discover if they are polite, sincere and knowledgeable in their craft. Some may inform you they are too busy, which is fine. It's better to know this earlier rather than later because you can then search for alternatives.

If not done before, you need to put time into due diligence on contractors before the tender process. If you move on to flipping further properties, it will be time well spent.

The tender process

Finding someone reputable to do the job you want takes time and effort, but it's an essential part of ensuring a successful renovation project. Don't rush into hiring the first tradesperson you come across – take the time to do your research and find someone who is reliable, experienced and has a good track record of completing similar projects to a high standard.

Getting estimates

For the tender process, it's worth inviting tenders from at least three contractors and interviewing them before making a decision. Ask for references and photographs of their previous work, and make sure that they have experience with projects similar to yours.

Ask each one to provide a written estimate outlining the scope of work, materials required and their fee structure. This will help you compare different people and ensure that you're getting a fair price. It is a good idea to give contractors a timeline (I suggest two weeks) to return quotes, based on the complexity or scale of the project. Always give them a fixed day and time to return the quote, for example Friday 30 June at 5pm.

The cheapest contractor is not always the best to go with as they may have cut corners to get the job. Make sure they have covered everything you want them to quote for and that they are available when you need them. Some contractors can leave essential items out so that they get the job and you are then left with a compromised design, so make sure the quotes are itemised so that you can compare them fairly.

Using sustainable contractors

Considering contractors with a sustainable approach to their work can have mutual benefits. These practices can greatly align your property flipping endeavours with current market trends, fostering responsible environmental practices, and can ultimately lead to greater financial success and social impact.

Look out for these key items to ensure your chosen contractor aligns to your sustainability values:

- **Prioritise eco-friendly practices:** Sustainable contractors prioritise using energy-efficient materials, reducing waste and employing green building techniques. By choosing such contractors, you can minimise the property's environmental impact and contribute to a more sustainable future.

- **Appeal to eco-conscious buyers:** As sustainability gains prominence in the property market, more buyers seek eco-friendly properties. Flipping a property with sustainable contractors helps makes it more attractive to eco-conscious buyers, increasing the chances of a quick and profitable sale.

- **Invite long-term cost savings:** Sustainable contractors often use energy-efficient materials and technologies that can lead to long-term cost savings for the property's future occupants. Energy-efficient appliances, lighting and insulation can lower utility bills, making the property more appealing to potential buyers.

- **Meet environmental regulations:** Sustainable contractors are often well-versed in the latest building codes and certifications related to eco-friendly construction. Working with them ensures that your property meets environmental regulations and qualifies for relevant green certifications, further enhancing its value.

- **Stand out from the crowd:** Sustainable contractors tend to stay up to date with the latest innovations in green building materials and techniques. By leveraging their expertise, you can incorporate cutting-edge, high-quality elements into the property, making it stand out in a crowded market.

- **Maintain value and demand:** A property with sustainable features and construction is likely to hold its value well over time. As more people prioritise sustainability in their living choices, properties with eco-friendly features may experience increased demand in the future.

Securing your contractors

When embarking on a house flipping project, it is crucial to have all your contractors in place and ready to go before you begin. This is because house flipping projects typically have tight timelines and require a high level of coordination between different trades and tasks. If you start your project without securing your contractors, you risk delays, cost overruns and poor-quality work.

By having your contractors in place before you start, you can ensure that you have the right team with the necessary skills and experience to complete your project on time and to a high standard. You can also avoid the stress and frustration of trying to find contractors at the last minute, which can be a daunting and time-consuming process.

Furthermore, having your contractors in place early on can help you better plan and budget for your project. You can get accurate quotes from each contractor, compare prices and quality of work, and negotiate terms before starting your project. This allows you to create a comprehensive project plan and avoid unexpected costs or delays that could hurt your profitability.

PROGRAMME OF WORKS

If you have a project manager or quantity surveyor, they will draw up the programme of works (the timeline for keeping the project on track), but you still need to understand it.

If you are managing the project yourself, this is an outline of works on a typical renovation in the required order.

- **Demolition:** Removing any existing structures or features that are being replaced or updated.
- **Structural work:** Any necessary modifications or repairs to the walls, roof or other structural components.

- **Plumbing and electrical work:** Installing new or updating existing plumbing and electrical systems.
- **Insulation:** Installing or updating insulation to improve energy efficiency and reduce heating and cooling costs.
- **Drywall and plastering:** Installing drywall or plaster and finishing it with joint compound or plaster.
- **Flooring:** Installing new flooring, which can include hardwood, tile, carpet or other materials.
- **Painting:** Including walls, ceilings and trims.
- **Fixed joinery:** Installing new cabinetry, countertops, sinks and other fixtures.
- **Final touches:** Installing any finishing touches, such as lighting, window treatments, staging and pre-property listing presentation.

Some of these steps may occur simultaneously or out of order, depending on the specific needs of the project. Some renovations may also require additional steps such as roof repairs, landscaping or exterior painting.

Summary

- Effective management of the renovation process is crucial for maximising ROI.
- Proper management ensures efficient utilisation of resources, including time, money and labour.
- Careful planning, budgeting and coordination are necessary for successful project execution.

- Hire contractors and subcontractors who are reliable and experienced and have a sustainable approach in their respective fields.
- Source materials and supplies from reputable suppliers to ensure quality and timely delivery.
- Obtain necessary permits and approvals to comply with local regulations.
- Oversee the project timeline and make adjustments as needed to avoid delays.
- Regularly monitor the progress of the renovation to ensure it aligns with the planned timeline and budget.
- Make informed decisions throughout the renovation process, considering the preferences and demands of the target market.
- Maintain a clear vision for the final outcome and communicate it effectively to the contractors and team members.
- Address any issues or challenges promptly to minimise disruptions and maintain project momentum.
- Regularly assess the progress and quality of the renovation work to ensure it meets the desired standards.
- Strive to maximise the property's appeal and potential resale value through strategic design choices and improvements.

- Keep open lines of communication with the contractors, team members and other stakeholders involved in the renovation.

- By effectively managing the renovation process you can minimise cost overruns, delays and setbacks, which can impact profits.

- Ultimately, maintaining a clear vision, monitoring progress and making informed decisions will optimise the outcome and secure the highest possible ROI when the property is sold.

7
Keys For Maximising Return On Investment

The goal in this chapter is to complete your renovation to a high standard with all essential works offering buyers a well-finished, attractive empty space full of potential. What decisions do you need to make to secure the best ROI?

Selecting the right areas of focus, sustainable finishes and materials is a crucial aspect of property flipping that can significantly impact the ROI of your project. If you get this final stage of the transformation right, you will enhance the property's visual appeal, add value and increase its overall marketability. Overlooking this stage can result in a lower ROI or even a loss on your investment.

When it comes to choosing appliances, sanitaryware or materials, it's important to consider not just their functional value but also the voice or character they create. Materials can evoke a particular feeling or atmosphere, and this can be an important consideration in choosing what to spend on. For example, natural materials like wood or stone can create a warm and inviting atmosphere, while glass or metal can create a sleeker and more modern feel. Investing in high-quality sustainable materials can communicate a sense of luxury and value, while cheap or poorly made materials can detract from the overall impression.

Having your end user and target demographic in sight is even more relevant now as it will help you decide on the voice you want to create and who you will appeal to in every decision you make.

Which rooms will give you the best ROI?

Before we delve into material selection, it's important to focus on the rooms that will provide the best ROI. Generally speaking, kitchens, shortly followed by bathrooms, tend to have the highest ROI in a house flip.

The kitchen

Often considered the heart of the home, this is a major draw for many buyers. Upgrading the kitchen with modern appliances, countertops, cabinets and flooring can significantly increase the value of the home for various reasons:

- **Functionality:** A well-designed kitchen with ample storage space and modern appliances can make cooking and entertaining easier and more enjoyable. Buyers are willing to pay a premium for a functional kitchen that meets their needs.
- **Aesthetic appeal:** The kitchen is a highly visible room that can make or break a buyer's first impression of the home. Upgrading the cabinets, countertops, flooring and lighting can give the kitchen a fresh and modern look, which can increase the home's overall value.
- **Resale value:** The kitchen is one of the most important rooms for resale value. Buyers are often willing to pay more for a home with an updated and well-appointed kitchen. This can translate to a higher ROI for the house flipper.

The bathroom

Bathrooms are also important to buyers, and a well-designed and updated bathroom can make a big difference in a home's overall value. Upgrades such as new fixtures, vanities, lighting and flooring can give a bathroom a fresh and modern look. Bathrooms can be renovated or upgraded relatively inexpensively compared to kitchens. New tiles, new fixtures and a fresh coat of paint can significantly improve the look of a bathroom without breaking the bank.

Reasons to spend on a bathroom:

- **Increase the property's value:** A functional bathroom is an essential part of any home. Potential buyers are likely to consider the number of bathrooms and their condition when making a purchasing decision. Therefore, renovating or upgrading a bathroom can significantly increase the value of a property.
- **Increase the property's appeal:** Bathrooms are one of the most used rooms in a house, and buyers will pay attention to their appearance. A well-designed and stylish bathroom can increase the overall appeal of a property, making it more attractive to potential buyers.
- **Recoup the cost:** According to *Remodelling* magazine, a mid-range bathroom remodel can recoup up to 66.7% of its cost upon resale (uplifting the value of the bathroom by 66.7%) in US Markets in 2023.[13]

What else will yield the biggest ROI?

Here's a list of priorities that are the most effective use of your budget.

---

13 '2023 Cost Vs Value Report', *Remodelling* (2023), https://remodeling.hw.net/cost-vs-value/2023, accessed 12 October 2023

Outstanding survey issues

It is essential to first address issues picked up in the survey, such as damp, structural problems and dodgy electrics. These concerns will only come up again when you sell, so address them now rather than having a buyer asking for money off during the sale.

Electricals

Updating the electrical system is always a wise investment. Old or faulty electrical systems can be a safety hazard and can also make the property less attractive to potential buyers. Upgrading to a modern electrical system can provide peace of mind to the new owners and reduce the risk of costly repairs down the line.

This can also increase the property's functionality and energy efficiency, attracting buyers who are looking for a modern, efficient property, contributing to a higher ROI.

Having a modern, safe electrical system can increase the property's overall value and make it more appealing to potential buyers, leading to a potentially higher selling price. Upgrading your switch sockets to chrome can also instantly add perceived quality to your property without costing a fortune.

Lighting

Adequate and appropriate lighting is important throughout. Installing energy-efficient lighting fixtures such as LED bulbs or recessed lighting can improve functionality and aesthetics.

In the kitchen, for example, if you have an island unit or dining area, decorative ceiling pendants can help elevate the space when you come to final presentation (more on this in the next chapter). Having good hallway lighting also helps to create a great first impression that buyers receive as they walk through the door.

In addition, many buyers today are more energy conscious and if the EPC shows efficiency, it can help in the sale.

Material world: When to invest in quality

Materials for kitchens and bathrooms

As mentioned earlier, these two rooms are most likely to give you your best ROI so it's best not to cut corners. It is worth choosing materials and appliances that are durable, visually appealing and within budget.

Remember to consider the overall style and design of the kitchen when selecting materials to ensure a cohesive and visually appealing look. It's also important to keep in mind the local market and price point of the property to ensure a good return on investment. Consider the following:

- **Kitchen units:** High-quality laminate cabinets are an excellent investment as they are long lasting and come in many different finishes to add value and appeal to your end user. Be cautious about choosing colourful cabinets –although these may be on trend in the kitchen showrooms, they can narrow your audience and date fast. Choose neutral colours or timber veneers. In a large kitchen, a darker grey can help ground the space.

- **Countertops:** One of the most noticeable features in a kitchen. Granite, quartz or marble countertops are popular choices that add both elegance and durability to the kitchen. Opting to salvage countertops, particularly those crafted from premium materials like quartz, can yield a savvy investment. By repurposing and reusing these durable surfaces, you not only contribute to sustainable practices but also tap into the inherent value of their quality. Choosing salvaged worktops not only showcases your commitment to responsible design but also offers a cost-effective way to enhance your kitchen's functionality and visual appeal.

- **Flooring:** Durable, attractive flooring options such as hardwood, ceramic tiles, luxury vinyl tiles (LVT) or planks are good choices. These are easy to maintain and can withstand heavy foot traffic and kitchen spillages.

- **Splashback:** This not only protects the walls from spills and stains but also adds a decorative element to a kitchen. Ceramic tiles or quartz are popular choices that are both durable and stylish.

- **Appliances:** Upgrading to energy-efficient appliances is a wise investment as it not only adds value to the property but also saves on energy costs in the long run. Brands such as Bosch or Neff stand proud in the appliance world and give the kitchen a high-end voice. If your budget doesn't stretch, reliable brands such as Lamona are a good back-up option. Remember that these items will increase your ROI, so see them as an investment, not an outlay.

If you are flipping a property to rent, items that will have longevity in both kitchens and bathrooms will minimise landlord management later.

Floors

Updating floor finishes is a great investment to consider. Old, worn-out flooring, especially carpets, can emit unpleasant odours that can turn buyers off instantly. Replacing carpets with new ones in a neutral colour or upgrading to hardwood, laminate or tile flooring can transform the property's overall look and feel, making it more inviting and modern. It can also improve the property's functionality, durability and maintenance, attracting buyers who are looking for a low-maintenance property.

Knobs and knockers

Touch points (literally, anything the prospective buyer is likely to touch when viewing your property, such as ironmongery, sanitaryware and front door knockers) are crucial to first impressions and need to be good quality to indicate a high-end finish and reflected end market price.

Painted surfaces

It may sound obvious but updating and freshening up the paintwork on walls, ceilings and woodwork is a cost-effective way to improve the kerb appeal and make a property more appealing when flipping on a budget. Old, worn-out paint can make the property look tired and uninviting, while fresh, modern paint can instantly make it feel cleaner and better maintained, making it stand out from other listings and attract potential buyers who are looking for a property with a modern, updated look. Cheaper paint may need more coats, costing time as well as money.

This is not the time for bright or bold colours, even if you love them. A neutral backdrop will give viewers a blank canvas and make it more appealing to your wider audience. There is an enormous range within the neutral palette, and you need to be aware of current trends. Avoid any colours with a yellow undertone. Even the word 'magnolia' sends a shiver through my bones! In the eighties and nineties this colour was used throughout most houses (our own included) and should be avoided if you want a fresh, contemporary look.

THE GOOD NEUTRAL GUIDE

A guide to neutral paint colours and the voice they can create:

- **White:** A bright white can create a crisp, clean look, while a softer white can create a warm, inviting feel.
- **Beige:** A warm beige can create a cosy, inviting feel, while a cooler beige can create a more modern, sophisticated look.
- **Grey:** A light grey can create a soft, calming feel.
- **Greige:** A mix of grey and beige, greige can create a versatile and neutral backdrop that can work with a variety of decor styles.
- **Taupe:** a neutral, brownish-grey colour with a subdued and timeless appearance.

Usable outside space

Check that you are making the most of whatever outside space you have, whether it's a roof terrace, a small patio or a full-blown garden. We'll explore external staging in the next chapter, but start by making it as presentable as possible.

Additions to consider include:

- **Outdoor table and chairs:** A simple seating area is usually all it takes to show the potential for entertaining or relaxing.
- **Sunloungers:** Leave these out if you're selling in the summer.
- **Trellis screens or tall planting:** Especially important if the space lacks privacy from neighbours.
- **Pot plants, window boxes and hanging baskets:** These make bare outdoor spaces more colourful and interesting without blowing your budget on landscape gardening.
- **Gravel or small stones:** For low-maintenance and a good-looking space.

Finishing touches

It is important to do the touching-up jobs before you are ready to put your property on the market to sell because first impressions matter. Even small imperfections such as chipped paint, scuffed floors or outdated fixtures can be a turn off and may lead to lower offers or fewer interested buyers. Touching up these areas can improve the overall appeal of the property and create a more positive impression, which can increase the likelihood of a sale and potentially lead to higher offers. This can save time and money in the long run, as buyers may request repairs or lower their offer based on the condition of the property.

Giving your property a thorough sparkle clean before putting it on to the market is a must for several reasons. First, a clean and tidy property is visually more appealing and attractive to potential buyers, which can increase the chances of receiving higher or even multiple offers. It will also create a positive first impression, giving potential buyers the impression that the property has been well maintained, upgraded and cared for. This can increase their confidence in the property and make them more likely to consider making an offer. Remember to remove all rubbish from the outside bins.

Kerb appeal: How first impressions last

First impressions start before potential buyers cross the threshold. Outside kerb appeal (what people see when they drive or walk past the property) is a huge factor in home sales. Lots of buyers 'drive by' a property to check whether it's worth their while booking a proper viewing appointment, so you need the same attention to detail outside as inside.

The front door

Despite what I said above about neutral colours, the rules change for exterior doors. Potential buyers will always remember the house with the cheerful turquoise door, so you don't need to be afraid of colour here.

Keep the front door area clean and tidy at all times. If you have a driveway, the only thing on show should be a clean car. Anything else will just detract attention from what you are trying to showcase.

Door ironmongery is the first touch point, so it is crucial that it looks great. Polish your door knocker and, if it's looking dated, replace it with something stylish or quirky. Make sure your doorbell works and doesn't look like it could give an electric shock!

Planters in a range of sizes and scale next to the front door can give a sense of transition between outside and in. Play with textures, teaming metal planters with terracotta to add interest. It's another great way of enticing the viewer in through the front door to see what's inside.

Other jobs to do if you have a front garden or driveway:

- Mow the lawn.
- Clip back and neaten any hedges.

- Keep the flowerbeds, driveways and paths weed free and sweep away dead leaves.

- Remove any plants that have died.

We'll explore property staging in the next chapter, but it's worth thinking about kerb appeal as soon as the messy renovation work has finished. If someone feels welcome and engaged before they walk through the door, you have their attention and are that much closer to a sale. Once people step inside the front door, they form an impression in 7–10 seconds... that's what we'll consider in the next chapter.

Summary

- Prioritise essential works and address structural issues, plumbing, electrical and roofing problems for safety and functionality.

- Enhance aesthetics by choosing durable, sustainable and visually appealing materials, flooring, paint colours, lighting and cabinetry to create an inviting space.

- Optimise layout and design by maximising square footage, optimising the floor plan, reconfiguring rooms and adding storage solutions.

- Research the target demographic and local property market and consider market trends to add value with popular features and amenities.

- Budget wisely and allocate funds strategically to achieve a balance between quality and cost-effectiveness to achieve a higher ROI.

8
On Your Marks, Get Set, Stage

You have done all the heavy lifting and the house is looking great... but it's empty. Selling an empty house can be an arduous task as it can lack the warmth and character of a fully furnished home, which can make it difficult for potential buyers to imagine themselves living there.

Over the past few months, you will have spent a lot of time and effort (and money) getting your property up to market standard. Why stop there and risk losing money on your sale by marketing it empty? Without furniture and soft furnishings, a house can appear smaller than it actually is, which can turn off some buyers. Flaws and imperfections, or maintenance issues such as peeling paint or worn flooring, can become more apparent in an empty house and some may need to be addressed before a sale can take place. The atmosphere of an empty house can also feel eerie and uninviting to potential buyers.

Property staging (using carefully chosen additions to make the space appeal to the lifestyle aspirations of buyers) is standard practice in the US. It has become increasingly popular in the UK in recent years as more and more sellers and estate agents recognise its potential to increase the value of a property. By creating an attractive, well-staged space, sellers can build a more emotional connection with potential buyers and highlight the best features of the property. This can ultimately lead to a quicker sale and a higher selling price.

In this chapter, we will explore the benefits of property staging, including how it can enhance the appeal of your property, increase its perceived value and help you to stand out in a competitive market. I will also provide practical tips and advice on how to stage your property effectively, from choosing the right furniture and accessories to making cosmetic improvements and creating a welcoming atmosphere. Whether you're a property flipper or a homeowner looking to sell, property staging is a powerful tool that can help you achieve your goals and maximise the value of your investment.

What is property staging?

Property staging is the process of preparing a property for sale by strategically arranging furniture, accessories and other items to enhance its appeal and make it more attractive to potential buyers. The goal of staging is to showcase the property's best features to create a welcoming, inviting environment that helps buyers to envision themselves living there. By staging a property, sellers can make it stand out in a competitive market, capture the attention of potential buyers and ultimately increase the likelihood of a quick, successful sale.

Staging a property before it goes on the market is highly recommended because it can significantly increase the chances of a successful sale. In my many years of experience in the business, I have found that there is a much higher success rate to go in full hit first time, rather than having a 'let's just see if it sells empty' attitude. In many cases, when this happens the property is sitting on the market unsold and it can create doubt in the viewers mind if it gets taken off the market only to be put back on staged.

When a property is left empty, it can be difficult for potential buyers to envision themselves living in the space, leading to a lack of emotional connection and interest. Emotion sells properties and an absence of this connection can create doubt in the eyes of viewers and ultimately result in a longer time on the market or even no sale at all.

A newly listed, well-staged property creates a positive first impression, generating excitement and a sense of urgency. By highlighting the best features of the property and creating a warm, inviting atmosphere, staging can help to attract potential buyers, ultimately leading to a quicker sale at a higher price.

You can hire professional stagers or take on the task yourself (for me, it's the most creative part of the flipping process), but even if you delegate it, you need to understand it.

How staging works

One of the primary benefits of property staging is its ability to highlight the positives and deemphasise the negatives of a property. By strategically arranging furniture and decor, you can draw attention to the property's best features, such as an open floor plan or a beautiful view, while downplaying an awkward layout or outdated fixtures. Potential buyers can then see the property in its best possible light and imagine themselves living there. Decluttering the space and creating a cohesive look and feel can help to create a sense of calm and order, which can also make a property more appealing to buyers and increase its perceived value.

Key elements in staging

Correctly scaled furniture that fits the proportions of each room can help to make a space feel bigger than it actually is, whereas oversized pieces can overwhelm a space and undersized pieces can make it feel empty and uninviting. By choosing furniture that is the appropriate scale for the room, you can create a sense of balance and harmony that makes the space feel larger and more open. Potential buyers visualise how their own furniture would fit in the space and how they would use each room.

By carefully selecting furniture and accessories that create a warm, inviting atmosphere – a group of lifestyle accessories including candles, a coffee jug and beautiful cups in a cosy corner next to an armchair, or an opened book and luxurious blankets and cushions on a window seat as a quiet reading nook away from the hustle and bustle of the family – you can help to evoke positive emotions in viewers, such as a sense of comfort, relaxation and inspiration. This emotional connection can help potential buyers to see the property as a home rather than just a physical space, creating a sense of attachment and desire that can ultimately lead to a quicker, more successful sale.

By creating a seamless transition from room to room and emphasising the unique character and charm of each space, property staging can help to create a cohesive and inviting environment that stands out in a competitive market. Creating a flow through the property is a critical aspect of effective staging, and it can have a significant impact on the overall market appeal and perceived value of the property. By cleverly arranging furniture and decor to create clear pathways and intuitive traffic flow, you can guide potential buyers through rooms in a certain order and maximise usable space. You will then show them the full potential of the property as you help them navigate the space and envision themselves living there.

A well-staged property can help to tap into buyers' aspirations and dreams, highlighting the potential lifestyle benefits of the property and creating a sense of excitement and anticipation. This emotional connection can be a powerful motivator for buyers, leading them to make an offer on the property and even pay a premium price.

Why stage a property?

Property staging is a powerful tool for creating the best possible first impression, both online and offline, when selling your property.

In today's digital age, the majority of buyers begin their property search online, and the first impression they form is based on the photographs and virtual tour of the property. A well-staged property can make a significant difference in the quality of these online listings, attracting more attention and clicks from potential buyers. By creating a visually appealing and inviting space, property staging can help to generate interest and encourage viewers to schedule a showing in person.

Property staging also plays a vital role in creating a positive first impression for buyers who visit the property in person. A well-staged property can create a warm and welcoming atmosphere that makes viewers feel comfortable and at home, allowing them to imagine themselves living there. This positive emotional connection can help to set the stage for a successful showing, increasing the likelihood of a sale.

Homeowners, flippers and estate agents can all benefit from property staging and the positive impact it can bring to their lives by selling quicker and for more money. In recent years, we have seen an influx of show homes on small developments by small developers using our staging services, which have catapulted the sale of their houses during the construction phase. These are often small developers without an in-house design department, and outsourcing a professional property stager to showcase one of the houses can save them a lot of money without the overhead costs of full-time design team members.

Your five-step staging roadmap

The five building blocks model that I use with clients of my property staging business will guide you through the process of staging your property yourself and ensure you are clear about your objectives if you decide to hire professionals, minimising the chances of making expensive changes.

The first three steps – discover, analyse and identify – are essential, even if you decide to delegate the styling process.

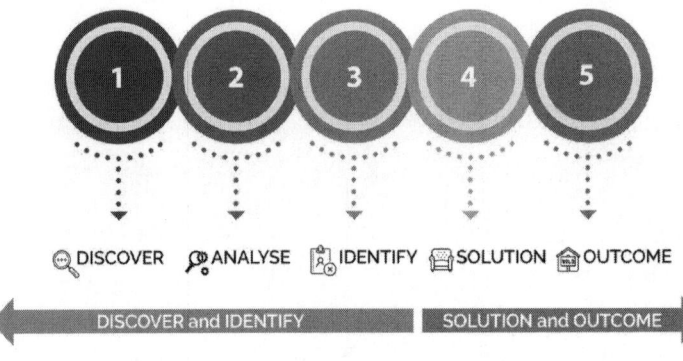

Five building blocks to elevate your assets

1. Discover

By discovering your overall outcome and goals, you will create a plan and strategy that aligns with your desired outcome. You can then tailor your staging efforts to meet your specific needs and objectives, whether you're looking to sell the property quickly or maximise its rental income potential.

If your primary goal is to sell the property quickly, you might focus on creating a neutral and clutter-free environment that allows potential buyers to visualise themselves living in the space. You may also emphasise the property's best features and highlight its unique selling points to make it stand out from the competition.

Alternatively, if your goal is to maximise rental income potential, you might focus on creating a luxurious and comfortable environment that appeals to high-end renters. You might add amenities and features that renters value, such as high-speed internet, modern appliances and smart home technology.

I encourage you to dig deep for this step and return to the 'why' analysis you completed in Chapter 1, considering your long-term as well as your short-term goals.

2. Analyse

If you have already put your property on the market as an empty space, get as much feedback as you can on why potential buyers didn't make an offer.

Understanding why your property isn't selling and what is putting viewers off is gold when it comes to property staging. There may be issues that have gone under your radar but can now be your priority to address.

If you have had feedback that the living room is too small for a family with two teenagers, think about making the largest/master bedroom into a teenager's room with a small sofa and hangout area to double the potential living room space of the house. Many parents will happily accept a smaller bedroom for less pressure on the shared living space. Perhaps there's an awkward corner in the kitchen or dining area that could be transformed into a reading nook, looking out on to the back garden.

Thinking outside the box is key to staging a property successfully, using clever furniture and accessory placement to show the viewer potential that they may not have thought about. This gives you the advantage over similar properties that buyers may be viewing.

3. Identify

In Chapter 4, I encouraged you to dig deep into who your target demographic audience is. By understanding their needs and preferences, staging is an excellent opportunity in which you can create a space that appeals to their lifestyle and interests. Here are some tips on how to stage a property to appeal to a specific target market:

- **Define the target market for the property:** Consider the demographic characteristics of potential buyers, such as age, income, lifestyle and family status.
- **Research the latest design trends and preferences of the target market:** For instance, if

the target market is a family with young children, consider adding child-friendly features, such as a playroom or a safe outdoor play area.

- **Create a focal point in each room:** This should showcase the property's best features and appeal to the target market. For example, if the target market is young professionals, consider creating a stylish and functional home office or a cosy reading nook.

- **Add personal touches that appeal to the target market:** Include artwork or accessories that reflect interests and hobbies particularly suited to that niche.

- **Choose furniture and accessories that align with the target market's preferences and lifestyle:** For instance, if the target market is older adults, consider incorporating comfortable seating and soft lighting to create a cosy and relaxing atmosphere.

- **Highlight amenities that are important to the target market:** For example, a spacious kitchen or a teenagers' hangout area. Fresh flowers and high-quality towels make bathrooms feel more luxurious and appealing.

- **Consider colour schemes:** Choose furniture and accessories that appeal to the target market's preferences and reflect the property's style and architecture – see my colour psychology guidelines from Chapter 7.

Step 4 of the building blocks model is the solution, my staging process. I'll talk you through this in detail. You'll see that the outcome, Step 5, speaks for itself.

4. My core staging process: The key tasks

The first impression of a property is crucial. Therefore, focus on creating an attractive and inviting exterior that will entice potential buyers. Ensure that the lawn is well-manicured, the driveway and pathway are clean, and the front porch and entryway are welcoming and clutter-free.

Identify the property's key features, such as a beautiful view, spacious bedrooms or a modern kitchen, and make them the focal point of each room. Use furniture and accessories to draw attention to these features and create an inviting atmosphere.

Remove any clutter, personal belongings and excessive furniture to make each room look more spacious and neutral. Believe it or not, the more furniture in a room, the smaller the space feels, which creates overwhelm. Instead, use suggestions such as a couple of stools and a simple place setting at a breakfast bar, rather than overcrowding the counter with too much clutter.

Natural light can make a room feel more spacious, inviting and vibrant. Consider opening the windows, using sheer curtains or adding mirrors to reflect the natural light.

Every room in the house should be staged, including bedrooms, bathrooms and living spaces. This will create a cohesive, inviting atmosphere that will entice potential buyers to imagine themselves living in the entirety of the space. Add finishing touches such as fresh flowers, candles and high-quality towels to create a luxurious and inviting atmosphere.

Neutral colours, such as white, beige and light grey, create a blank canvas that allows potential buyers to imagine how they would personalise the space. Consider using neutral colours on walls, furniture and decor to create a cohesive, inviting atmosphere and backdrop, perfect for adding pops of colour and texture with soft furnishings and accessories.

STAGE LIKE A PRO

Professional property stagers use a variety of tricks to create a visually appealing and inviting space that appeals to a wider range of potential buyers. Here are some tricks that deliver success:

- **Add mirrors:** These can make a space feel larger and brighter by reflecting light and creating the illusion of more space. This is particularly important in entrance halls and lobbies. As soon as the viewer steps into your property they will instantly see themselves there, which can be a powerful tool in creating emotion.

- **Stage a celebration:** In the kitchen (usually one of the first areas viewers are drawn to), have a bottle of champagne and two glasses in view on the countertop. This will subconsciously evoke a feeling of celebration in the viewers' minds that they have successfully bought the property of their dreams!
- **Create zones:** Use furniture and rugs to create distinct zones in open-plan living spaces to help potential buyers understand how the space can be used. Rugs should be used to 'ground' the furniture and should always be large enough for the front two legs of each chair and sofa to be on.

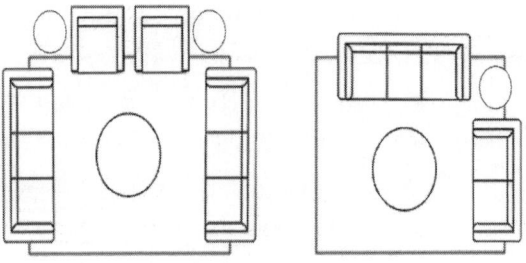

Zoning for success

- **Make rooms appear larger:** Choose furniture that is appropriately scaled to the size of the room to create a sense of balance and proportion. This can also help to make the space feel larger and more open.
- **Highlight unique features of the property:** Emphasise a quiet reading nook or a high ceiling with appropriate lighting and accessories.
- **Use artwork and accessories to add interest and depth:** This can be achieved through a mix of

layering colour, texture and pattern in furniture and accessories.
- **Make the most of lighting:** Use strategically placed lighting to create ambience and highlight key features of the space.
- **Add plants and flowers:** This will create a sense of warmth and life to the space, as well as helping to purify the air and create a calming environment.
- **Create a visual flow:** Choose a cohesive design style and colour scheme throughout the property. This can help to create a sense of harmony and balance.

Why hire a professional?

You may feel confident to manage the staging yourself, which is great, but bringing in a professional stager can have so many added benefits. Professional stagers are trained to look at a home objectively, identify its strengths and weaknesses and suggest ways to highlight its best features, which you may not have noticed yourself.

Professional stagers have experience in designing and arranging spaces to create an appealing and functional layout. They know how to make a home look its best by using furniture, accessories and lighting to create a cohesive, welcoming environment. They also understand the local property market and know what buyers are looking for. They can use this knowledge to create a staging plan that will appeal to potential buyers in the area.

Staging a home can be time consuming, especially if you're not sure what you're doing. Professional stagers can take care of everything, from selecting furniture to arranging accessories, freeing up your time to focus on other aspects of the home-selling process. There is no need to store furniture or schedule delivery dates for items. Neither is there any need to work out the best placement of furniture, assemble it, or lug accessories back and forth, learning how to place them for maximum impact or having to return items that aren't quite right. These can be time-consuming exercises; time that could be used to search for your next property to flip as soon as your current one has sold.

Professional stagers can help to increase the value of your home and attract more potential buyers, which can lead to a higher selling price – without any of the hassle. The best part is that, in most cases, the cost of professional staging can be offset by the increased sale price of the home.

Sustainable staging

Sustainability is one of the core values of my business and incorporating these practices into our staging projects is always at the forefront of our minds. Here's how we do it and how you can easily incorporate it into your DIY approach:

- **Natural materials:** Use sustainable, renewable materials like bamboo, reclaimed wood or recycled glass for furniture and decorative pieces.

- **Second-hand and upcycled furniture:** Incorporate this to reduce waste and showcase creative reuse.

- **Indoor plants:** Integrate indoor plants for a touch of nature and improved air quality. This aligns with a sustainable, healthy living environment.

- **Minimalist design:** Adopt a minimalist approach to staging to showcase open spaces and highlight the property's natural features, with less need for clutter.

- **Educational material:** Provide brochures or information sheets about the property's sustainable features and their benefits to potential buyers.

- **Green cleaning:** Use eco-friendly cleaning products to maintain a clean and healthy living environment during showings.

5. The value property staging adds

Property staging is still an upcoming industry in the UK and a new concept for many UK developers and flippers. When I introduce the idea I often get counter-arguments like the following, to which there are some compelling answers in favour of property staging:

- **'I can sell my property without staging':** You think the problem is that the market is quiet and that is why your property isn't selling. The real problem is viewers can't imagine how to live in a large empty space. It's true that your property will eventually sell… it's just a matter of when and for how much. Even if your property sells quickly in a good market, it doesn't mean that it sold for the top amount it could have commanded with professional staging. Remember, professionally staged homes sell on a conservative average for about 6%+ more than nonstaged homes. If your home sold for £300K unstaged, it probably would have sold for £320K staged.

- **'My property is in a great area and it will sell quickly anyway':** That's true too, but why wouldn't you give your property the best chance possible to get more viewers and – ultimately what everyone wants – a speedy closing date and a higher offer? Why not invest 5K to make 10K?

- **'My property has just been refurbished; it will sell itself':** If it's still an empty space, most viewers don't have the vision to imagine what it could be. If you don't have that eye, empty space = overwhelm. Overwhelm = excuses not to buy. In staging your property well, you are doing the thinking for your buyer.

- **'Property staging is just another outlay that I can do without. I just want to get my property sold':** Shift your mindset to see property staging as an investment into your own hard work so far, rather than a drain. Statistics show that a professionally staged home will command a higher price than a vacant property. As Movewise reports: 'Home staging costs 0.5–1.0% and offers an expected price increase of 3.0%. That's a massive 300% to 600% return on the cost of staging in less than six months.'[14]

The positive feedback I have received from clients shows that property staging works:

- **'We have sold the property in record time':** No longer living in 'limbo land', you can move on with your life and be free of this burden which has been hanging over your head. It gives you the freedom and opportunity to enjoy life again.

- **'We have sold the property for 15% above the asking price':** All your financial worries have gone and you have made a great profit on your investments. You have financial freedom, reassurance that you have made the right decisions and the confidence that you will have a successful property developer business with a good source of income.

- **'We have sold our property quickly with a great ROI and profit':** All your hard work has paid off and you are now able to move on to your

---

14 Stage Your Home to Sell Faster and Secure the Best Price, *Movewise*, https://movewise.co.uk/articles/stage-your-home-to-sell-faster-and-secure-best-price, accessed 12 October 2023.

next investment opportunity and grow your property development business faster than you ever imagined. You have the empowerment that you have made the right decision to become a respected property developer and you are back in charge of your own destiny.

CASE STUDY: Staging for success

A property developer couple we worked with had spent thousands of pounds and a lot of time and energy renovating their two-bedroom, semi-detached house in the suburbs of Manchester, only to have it sitting on the market for months as an empty property. The finishes were immaculate with neutral-coloured walls, quartz worktops in the kitchen and a brand-new family bathroom. They couldn't understand why it wasn't selling and desperately needed to free up their capital ready to buy the next investment at auction. The couple had both spent time in the US during their corporate career as medical practitioners and were aware of staging as a standard tool employed to sell properties.

When they hired us, we immediately ascertained the features putting viewers off (the small lounge and separate small kitchen).The area had good local primary schools, so we decided to stage the property for a young family or couple about to start a family. We staged a bedroom as not only a potential spare room but also a nursery or child's bedroom (single bed, occasional chair, neutral colours, with bright, child-friendly accessories).

The day the property went back on the market, the couple received fourteen offers on the first day of viewing and they told us: 'We believe your magic has helped show off the house's full potential.'

This case study illustrates how property staging can have a profound impact on increasing the value of a property. By strategically arranging furniture and having a thorough grasp of the target audience, we successfully maximised the property's potential and showcased the improved lifestyle it could offer to potential viewers. The staging efforts resulted in heightened interest, expedited the sales process and ultimately led to a successful sale at a higher price.

Summary

- Staging is an essential step in the flipping to sell process that can greatly impact the success of the sale.

- A properly sustainably staged property can help potential buyers see themselves living in the space, highlight the property's best features, and differentiate it from other properties on the market.

- Failing to stage a property can result in a lack of interest from potential buyers, a longer time on the market and potentially lower offers.

- It is crucial to take the time and effort and make allowances in your budget to stage a property flip before putting it on the market.

PART THREE
GETTING IT SOLD

9
Selling The Lifestyle

In today's digital age, the vast majority of homebuyers begin their search online and rely on the listings to narrow down their choices before they set foot in a property. High-quality property photographs are therefore essential to attract potential buyers. Captivating and professional-looking images can make all the difference in capturing a buyer's attention and enticing them to schedule a viewing.

Getting things right when it comes to photographing your property flip can mean the difference between a quick sale at a desirable price and having your property languish on the market for months, so it's worth investing your time, energy and resources at this stage of the project to ensure that your property is presented in the best possible light. After all, you will have spent a significant amount of time and money renovating it.

In this chapter, we'll be delving into the intricacies of property photography to help you present your property flip in the best way possible. We'll be exploring the differences between photographs taken by professional photographers, those taken by estate agents and a DIY approach, highlighting why professional photographs are a worthwhile investment. We'll take you through the process of sourcing a good photographer, discussing key factors to consider and outlining what to expect from a professional shoot. Additionally, we'll provide tips on how to take captivating photos of your property yourself, highlighting key techniques and approaches to showcase your property's features and appeal to potential buyers. By the end of this section, you'll have a comprehensive understanding of how to create stunning property photographs that help sell your property flip at the best possible price.

Professional photography vs estate agents' services

While most estate agents offer property photography services as part of their package, investing in a professional photographer can make all the difference in the quality and effectiveness of your property listing. Estate agent photos are often taken using a wide-angle lens, which can make the space look bigger, but may not capture the details and personality that make your property stand out. In contrast, professional photographers have the technical expertise and creative vision to capture the essence your property offers, showcasing its unique features and creating an emotional connection with potential buyers. Remember that you are showcasing the lifestyle that the property represents, especially if you have worked hard on staging.

My good friend Oliver Kersh, who is a professional interiors photographer (www.photo-property.com), recommends that a great photographer will capture the balance of maximising the space and showcasing a lifestyle within their photographs for online listings. This offers a two-fold benefit by making the property look spacious (extremely valuable in real estate terms) and stirring up emotion in the viewer. He explains:

> 'A professional photographer views the property through a photographer's lens and understands what needs decluttering. Many homeowners cannot discern the difference, and this can distract potential buyers when they view the property.
>
> 'Many DIY photographers believe that shooting from both high and low angles will capture more in the photo. This approach has the opposite effect and can make the room appear smaller. Professional photographers

understand the precise eye-level height to maximise the sense of space in the image.'

Professional photographers know how to play with lighting, composition and angles to create captivating photographs that highlight your property's best features and showcase its potential. They can also give your property flip a sense of luxury, exclusivity and sophistication, making it stand out in a crowded online market. By investing in professional photographs, you're sending a clear signal to potential buyers that you're serious about selling and that you've taken the time and effort to present your property in the best possible light.

Ultimately, professional photographs can help you attract more serious buyers, sell your property more quickly and get a higher price, making the investment in a professional photographer worthwhile – which is even more important if the current market is slow.

How to source a professional photographer

Sourcing a good professional photographer for your property flip can be a daunting task, but with some research and careful consideration, it's possible to find a great photographer who can capture your property's essence and showcase it in the best possible light.

Firstly, it's important to look for a photographer with experience in property photography and a portfolio of work that showcases their abilities. You can find such photographers through recommendations from friends or colleagues, online searches, or by asking local property stagers and estate agents for referrals. Once you have a shortlist of potential photographers, check out their reviews and testimonials and compare their rates and services.

It's also important to consider their communication skills, responsiveness and professionalism, as these factors can significantly impact the quality of the final product. Additionally, it's essential to discuss your requirements and expectations with the photographer to ensure they understand your vision and can deliver the results you're looking for.

Ultimately, the key to sourcing a good professional photographer for your property flip is to do your research, communicate effectively and choose someone whose portfolio and approach align with your needs and expectations.

Key questions to ask a photographer

You have found a great photographer who ticks all your boxes, but what happens next?

Before the day of the shoot with a professional property photographer, it's important to ask the right questions to ensure that you are both on the same page and that the final photographs meet your expectations. Here are some questions you may want to consider asking:

- **What is your experience in photographing properties?** It's important to ensure that the photographer you choose has experience in photographing properties and has a portfolio of similar work to showcase their skills and style.

- **What equipment do you use for property photography?** Knowing the equipment used can give you an idea of the quality of the images and if the photographer has the necessary tools to capture your property in the best light. You don't have to be an expert in this area, but it will give you the tools to do your own research if you feel the need to do so. It also gives the message that you mean business and are willing to invest the time in getting things right from the outset.

- **How do you approach capturing the property's best features?** A professional photographer should have a strategy to capture the best features of your property, including lighting and angles, to create the most visually appealing images.

- **What is your editing process like?** Editing is an essential part of the photography process. It's important to understand the photographer's approach to editing and what they can do to enhance the final product.

- **How long will the shoot take and when will I receive the finished photos?** It's important to know the time frame for the shoot and when you can expect the final photos to be delivered. This can help you plan your marketing strategy and ensure that your listing goes live as planned.

- **Do you have any recommendations for preparing the property for the shoot?** A professional photographer may have specific recommendations to help you prepare your property for the shoot, such as staging (if you haven't already done this) to ensure that the final images look their best.

By asking these questions, you can ensure that you are working with a professional photographer who understands your expectations and can deliver high-quality images that showcase your property to its fullest potential.

Key questions a photographer should ask you

Before a shoot, the photographer will (or should) ask:

- **What is the property's address?** This is important information for the photographer to plan the logistics of the shoot and ensure they arrive at the correct location.

- **What type of property is it?** The photographer may ask if the property is a house, apartment, commercial space or other type of property to determine the appropriate equipment and techniques needed to capture the best photos.

- **What are your expectations for the shoot?** The photographer will likely ask about your goals for the photoshoot, such as highlighting specific features or capturing a certain ambience. This will help them understand what type of shots to focus on.

- **Are there any specific areas or features of the property that you want to highlight?** This could include specific rooms, architectural details or outdoor spaces. By understanding what you want to highlight, the photographer can ensure that those areas are given special attention during the shoot.

- **Is there anything unique or special about the property?** If there are unique or special features about the property, such as a beautiful view or historic architecture, the photographer may want to make sure they capture these elements.

- **What is the timeline for the photos to be delivered?** The photographer may ask about the timeline for the final images to be delivered so they can ensure they have enough time to edit and deliver the final product within the given time frame.

The day of the shoot

On the day of the shoot with a professional photographer, there are several things you can expect to ensure the process goes smoothly and produces the best possible results.

The photographer will arrive with their equipment and any necessary lighting or props, ready to set up and begin the shoot. They may ask for a tour of the property to assess the best angles and lighting for each room and discuss any specific shots or features that you want to highlight.

Once the shoot begins, they will take a range of shots from different angles and positions, capturing the property's essence and unique features. Depending on the size of the property, the shoot may take a few hours to complete, and the photographer may need to move furniture or adjust lighting to get the perfect shot. Communication with the photographer is crucial during the shoot, so you can work together to achieve the desired outcome.

After the shoot, the photographer will review and select the best images, edit them to enhance their appeal, and provide you with the final images for use in your online listing.

DIY photography

If you have time to invest, it can be possible to get decent results yourself. If you decide to take on the task yourself, first and foremost, the timing of the photography is crucial to capturing the most effective shots. The ideal time to photograph an interior of a property is during daylight hours, specifically when the light is at its best. Natural light provides a softer, more even and natural-looking illumination, enhancing the appeal of a space and bringing out its best features. Generally, mid-morning or mid-afternoon is the best time to capture interior photographs as the sun's position is less harsh and direct. This is often called the 'golden hour'.

It's essential to consider the orientation of the property and the direction of the windows to ensure you capture the best natural light. South-facing windows tend to receive more sunlight and provide the best light for capturing interior photographs.

How to take great interior photos on your smartphone

1. **Shoot down the centre:** Shooting straight down the middle is an excellent option when it comes to interior photography composition. Point your camera so that it properly lines up with one of your walls, using the room's architectural framework as a reference. In this way, the room's

horizontal and vertical components might be used as a sort of framework.

2. **Clear the clutter:** Your objective is to take a picture that captures the lifestyle your property can bring to the viewer. Make sure the things you want to see are the focal point of the photo and remove anything else. As professional stagers, we often use props such as a designer magazine, a coffee percolator and a vase of fresh flowers in a single colour.

3. **Move things around:** It's often a good idea to move large furniture pieces around to achieve the best composition and visual appeal in your photos. For example, a sofa or a chair might be blocking your view or obstructing the flow of the room and moving them will create a more open and inviting space. You might move a sofa to create a more natural focal point, or remove a chair to create more visual space in a room.

Professional vs DIY photos

While you can take successful photos of your property for an online listing yourself, there are significant advantages to hiring a professional photographer. A professional photographer can bring a level of expertise, equipment and editing skills that most individuals may not have, resulting in more captivating, high-quality photos that can attract potential buyers.

They can help to showcase the unique features and lifestyle your property offers, giving a better representation of the property to potential buyers.

While it may be tempting to take photos of the property yourself to save money, investing in a professional photographer can be money well spent. They have all the equipment, skills and experience needed to capture the best possible images of your property, which can save you a lot of time and attract more potential buyers, ultimately leading to a faster sale at a higher price point.

By showcasing the unique features and lifestyle your property offers through high-quality photos, you can give potential buyers a better sense of what it would be like to live in your property, which can be a powerful selling point. While it may be seen as an additional expense, it's worth considering a professional photographer as a necessary investment in the success of your property sale.

CASE STUDY: Adding value to a property through professional photography:

In this case study, I will examine how the involvement of our professional photographer Oliver significantly increased the value and market appeal of a property. Through his expertise and artistic skills, and in collaboration with the staging, he was able to capture captivating visuals that showcased the property in its best light and attracted potential buyers.

Property details

The property in question was a charming three-bedroom bungalow located in a small village just outside of Halifax in Yorkshire, with a quaint ambience and picturesque surroundings. While the property had unique features, such as a beautifully landscaped garden and original architectural details, it had struggled to generate substantial interest among potential buyers.

Engaging our professional photographer

Recognising the potential of the property but aware of the need for impactful visual representation, the homeowner decided to enlist the services of our professional photographer, with his reputation for capturing the essence and character of properties making him the ideal choice for the task.

The photography process

Upon arrival at the property, Oliver conducted a comprehensive assessment of its distinctive attributes, paying close attention to architectural details, natural lighting and standout features. Collaborating with myself who had staged the property, we discussed the property's selling points and the desired target market to tailor the photography accordingly.

During the shoot, Oliver used high-quality equipment and his expertise to compose each shot meticulously. He strategically selected angles, adjusted lighting and framed each photograph to highlight the property's most appealing aspects. He expertly captured the warm, inviting atmosphere, emphasising the cosy interior spaces and the harmonious connection between indoor and outdoor living areas.

The photographs

His photography had an immediate and transformative effect on the property's marketability. The visually stunning images became the centrepiece of the online listing, instantly attracting increased attention and engagement from potential buyers. The photographs showcased the property's distinct features, creating a strong desire among viewers to experience the cosy ambience for themselves.

The results

As a direct result of the combined professional photography and staging, the property received multiple offers within a short period. The competitive interest led to a successful sale at 8% higher than the original asking price of £295,000, giving the seller a clear £23,600 profit – minus the £300 photographer fee. The added value brought by our photographer played a significant role in attracting qualified buyers, creating a sense of urgency and ultimately maximising the property's selling price.

This case study demonstrates the transformative power of professional photography in adding value to a property. Through his skillful composition and artistic vision, Oliver was able to capture the unique charm and character of the bungalow, effectively showcasing its potential to buyers. The visually captivating images generated increased interest, accelerated the sales process and led to a successful sale at an enhanced price.

Summary

- Investing in professional photography can be a game changer for homeowners and property professionals.

- By harnessing the expertise of a skilled photographer, properties can be portrayed in their best light, attracting a wider audience, creating emotional connections and driving increased interest.

- In the competitive property market, professional photography has become an essential tool for adding value and maximising the appeal of a property.

10
Sealing The Deal

In this chapter, we will delve into the world of real estate and explore the process of choosing a good estate agent to assist you in the sale of your property. We will also discuss a DIY method that can help you bring in the maximum price for your property flip. As I know from my own experience, selling a property can be an intimidating task, and choosing the right estate agent is crucial to ensure a successful transaction. Furthermore, understanding the techniques that can help you maximise your profit when selling your property can be extremely beneficial.

Whether you decide to enlist the help of a professional or take matters into your own hands, this chapter will provide valuable insights and tips to help you sell your property efficiently and effectively.

Estate agents vs DIY selling

While a DIY approach may seem appealing due to the potential cost savings, there are many benefits to using an estate agent to sell your property flip. Firstly, estate agents have experience in selling properties and a solid understanding of the local real estate market. They can provide valuable advice on pricing, marketing and negotiating; all of which can significantly impact the success of the sale.

Estate agents have access to a wide network of potential buyers, including those who may be interested in your property but are not actively looking on property portals. They also have access to professional marketing tools, such as virtual tours and social media advertising, which can significantly increase the visibility and appeal of your property to potential buyers.

Using an estate agent can save you time and effort, as they can handle the majority of the sales process, including viewings, negotiations and paperwork. Finally, estate agents are experts in negotiating and can help you achieve the best possible price for your property. In contrast, a DIY approach may result in a lack of knowledge of the market, reduced access to potential buyers, and limited marketing resources, which can lead to a slower sale and a lower sale price.

Having an estate agent who is on board with your expectations is critical as it can make the difference between a successful sale and a frustrating experience. It's essential to choose an estate agent who understands your goals and is willing to work with you to achieve them.

Estate agents can help you set a realistic price that reflects the value of your property and the current market conditions, avoiding a disappointing outcome. Additionally, a good estate agent can provide valuable feedback on the presentation of your property, and any necessary last-minute improvements that can be made to increase its appeal to potential buyers, making the process a successful and rewarding experience. They will also organise an open day for your property and start talking to prospective buyers to gain momentum and excitement before it actually goes on the market.

Using an estate agent to sell your property flip can provide you with a faster, more efficient and ultimately more successful sale than the DIY approach.

Viewings

Deciding whether to conduct house viewings yourself or with an estate agent is another important consideration. While there are benefits to both approaches, there are also potential risks and challenges to consider. Conducting viewings yourself may seem appealing, as it allows you to showcase your property to potential buyers in a more personal and authentic way. You have the advantage of knowing your property better than anyone else, and you can highlight its unique features and lifestyle benefits. Additionally, it can save you money, as you won't have to pay an estate agent to conduct them.

There are potential risks and challenges associated with conducting viewings yourself. You may not have the same level of experience and knowledge as an estate agent when it comes to conducting viewings, which can result in a less effective and potentially awkward viewing experience. It can also be time consuming, particularly if you have a lot of interest in your property. On the other hand, using an estate agent to conduct viewings on your behalf will save you a lot of time and effort. They will guide a potential buyer around the property in line with the 'flow', which maximises the selling opportunity.

Overall, using an estate agent to conduct viewings can provide an added layer of safety and security, as they can vet potential buyers and ensure that only genuine and serious buyers view your property.

Offers and counter offers

The process of offers and counter offers is a common negotiation technique used when selling a property. It typically starts with a buyer making an initial offer on the property, which the seller can either accept or reject. If the offer is rejected, the buyer may make a second, improved offer, known as a counter offer. The seller can then choose to accept, reject or make a counter offer of their own. This process can continue until an agreement is reached, or until one party decides to walk away from the negotiation.

Summary

The advantages of enlisting an estate agent are:

- You can use their expertise, resources and market knowledge.
- They have the ability to navigate the complexities of the property market.
- You can benefit from enhanced marketing and exposure to the market.
- Buyer interest increases, resulting in successful sales.
- It is a valuable outsource for novice flippers.

The challenges of selling your property independently include:

- Limited market insights.
- Ineffective marketing strategies.
- Difficulties in viewings.

11
Preparing To Fly

By following the steps outlined in this book, you now have a seamless approach to flipping properties on a multiple scale. You will have gained valuable knowledge in finding and evaluating properties, creating accurate budgets and executing successful renovations. You'll also have learned effective marketing and selling strategies that will help you maximise your profits.

With this newfound expertise, you are now able to scale up your property flipping business to the next level and will be able to confidently take on larger projects, and manage multiple properties at once, while avoiding the common pitfalls that many flippers encounter.

By implementing all the *Flip and Fly* strategies and techniques, you have now set yourself up for long-term success in the competitive world of property flipping. With dedication, hard work and a commitment to excellence, you can achieve your goals and take your business to new heights.

The five-, ten- and twenty-year plan

As you continue to grow and develop your business, it is essential to remember the goals you worked on in Chapter 2 and to update them regularly. With your newfound knowledge and experience in the world of property flipping, you will have a clearer and more aligned vision of what you are now able to achieve in five, ten and twenty years from now.

You will have a better understanding of the market and the potential opportunities that exist, and a clearer idea of the resources and skills you need to achieve your goals. Updating your goals regularly will help you stay focused and motivated and ensure that you are taking the necessary steps to achieve your vision. It will also help you identify new opportunities and adjust your strategy as needed, allowing you to stay ahead of the curve and take advantage of emerging trends in the market.

By keeping your goals up to date and aligned with your new knowledge and experience, you can achieve greater success and fulfilment in your property flipping business over the long term.

The joy of outsourcing

By following the step-by-step process outlined in this book, you now have the tools to scale up your property flipping business quickly and efficiently. With a solid foundation of knowledge and experience, you can take on larger projects and manage multiple properties at once. As your business grows, you may find that you need to start outsourcing work to free up your time and focus on the aspects of the business that you enjoy the most.

Outsourcing can include tasks such as project management, marketing, bookkeeping and more. By delegating these tasks to others, you can focus on the areas of the business where your expertise is most valuable and use your time more effectively. This can also help you avoid burnout and maintain a healthy work-life balance. By scaling up your business and outsourcing work, you can achieve greater success and enjoy the freedom to do the things you love.

Effective delegation

Effective delegation of tasks is crucial for scaling up your property flipping business and freeing up your time to focus on the aspects of the business where your expertise is most valuable. It is one of the areas I struggled with when starting in my business. Over time, I have learned some key elements in how to do this efficiently and effectively, without compromising on your core values and high levels of expectation.

These include:

- **Having clear communication:** Ensuring that the person you are delegating tasks to understands what is expected of them, and that they have the necessary resources and information to complete the task.
- **Trust:** That the person you are delegating tasks to has the necessary skills and experience to complete the task to a high standard.
- **Accountability:** Setting clear deadlines and following up regularly to ensure that tasks are completed on time and to the required standard.
- **Flexibility:** Being open to new ideas and approaches to completing tasks and willing to adjust your approach as needed.
- **Providing constructive feedback on the completed task:** Using it as an opportunity for growth and development.

By following these key elements of effective delegation, you can ensure that tasks are completed efficiently and to a high standard, freeing up your time and eliminating stress, leaving you to focus on growing your business and achieving your goals. Effective delegation can also help build trust and confidence among your team, leading to increased motivation and productivity over time.

Building professional relationships

Building strong relationships with suppliers, buyers and estate agents can be incredibly beneficial for your property flipping business over time.

Suppliers can provide you with quality materials at a reasonable price, which can help you keep your costs down and increase your profits. This can also lead to preferential treatment and better terms in the long run.

Buyers – in all forms, such as property sources, landlords and buying agents – are the key to selling your properties quickly and for a good price. By building a good relationship with them, you can establish trust and credibility, which can make it easier to close deals and negotiate favourable terms. Repeat buyers can also provide a steady stream of business and referrals, which can help your business grow over time.

Estate agents can be a valuable source of information about the local property market and can help you find suitable properties to flip. By building a good relationship with estate agents, you can establish yourself as a serious buyer and gain access to off-market properties that may not be available to the general public. Estate agents can also help you sell your properties quickly and for a good price, by leveraging their network and marketing expertise. One of the best ways to build great relationships with agents and get access to off-market properties is to give them some of your existing rental properties to manage (if this is available).

Over time, these relationships can help you establish a strong and profitable business in the competitive world of property flipping.

Using checklists can also help to ensure that nothing is missed during the development process. Checklists can help to keep everyone on track and ensure that all tasks are completed on time and to the required standard. By employing a team of professionals and using checklists, you can create a more efficient, streamlined process for property development. This can help to save time, reduce costs and ensure that the project is completed to the highest possible standard.

CASE STUDY: Creating lasting wealth for a first-time property flipper

This case study highlights the remarkable journey of a first-time property flipper who has achieved lasting wealth through meticulous due diligence and effective implementation of key strategies. By conducting thorough research, engaging professionals, delegating tasks, adhering to budgetary constraints and leveraging expert services such as staging and photography, this individual has consistently achieved successful outcomes in property flipping.

Background

I first met Phil when we were enlisted to stage his two-bedroom property in Whitefield, a suburb not far out of Manchester, back in 2019. Since then, we have staged many of his properties and have become good friends in the process.

Phil is a novice investor with a keen interest in property. He embarked on his property flipping venture three years ago. Despite having limited experience, he recognised the potential profitability of this market and decided to dive in. Phil understood the importance of implementing a robust plan and sought to acquire the necessary skills and knowledge to excel in this field.

Due diligence and property selection

Before making any property purchase, Phil thoroughly conducted due diligence. He meticulously researched the local market trends, analysed property values and identified potential target areas. By studying the market and assessing various properties, he aimed to find undervalued assets with substantial potential for improvement.

Engaging professionals

Recognising the significance of expert advice, he enlisted the services of professionals such as architects and quantity surveyors. An architect helped him assess the structural integrity of potential properties, identify renovation possibilities and create appealing designs to enhance the overall aesthetics. The QS provided accurate cost estimates, ensuring that the budget was effectively managed throughout the renovation process.

Effective task delegation

Understanding the importance of efficient project management, Phil skilfully delegated tasks to qualified professionals and contractors. By entrusting skilled individuals with specific responsibilities, he ensured that each aspect of the flip was carried out to the highest standards. This enabled him to focus on overseeing the project, making informed decisions and coordinating the various activities involved.

Establishing ceiling price and budget adherence

To maintain profitability, Phil established a ceiling price for each property purchase. He diligently analysed the potential resale value after renovation and set a limit to avoid overinvesting. By adhering to a well-defined budget, he was able to control costs, avoid unnecessary expenses and optimise his returns.

Professional staging and photography

Phil understood the importance of creating an appealing visual presentation to attract potential buyers. For every property, he engaged us to skilfully arrange furniture and accessories to showcase the full potential and appeal of the space. Furthermore, he hired our professional photographer Oliver to capture high-quality images that highlighted the property's best features. This attention to detail significantly enhanced the marketing efforts and increased buyer interest.

Results and achievements

Phil's strategic approach and diligent execution of these key strategies have yielded impressive results. He has successfully flipped multiple properties within the last three years, consistently achieving profitable sales. By implementing due diligence, engaging professionals, delegating tasks effectively, adhering to budget constraints and utilising expert services for staging and photography, he has created lasting wealth through all his property flipping endeavours.

Conclusion

This case study showcases how a first-time property flipper, through meticulous planning and strategic implementation, has achieved lasting wealth. Phil has consistently achieved successful outcomes in property flipping, which demonstrates the potential for aspiring investors to build wealth through well-informed decision making and a comprehensive approach to property flips and sales.

Flying high to the next level

Growing your property flipping business can be the key to achieving the financial freedom you dream of. By taking advantage of the knowledge and experience gained from flipping properties, you can expand your business and ultimately generate a lot more income. As your business grows, you will have the ability to take on more projects and manage a larger team, which will of course lead to increased profits and greater financial stability.

This newfound financial freedom means that you no longer have to work in the nine-to-five grind, and you can be in control of your destiny and lifestyle. You can choose to work as much or as little as you like and enjoy the freedom to pursue other interests or spend more time with family and friends. Growing your property flipping business can open up a world of possibilities, allowing you to live life on your own terms and achieve the financial freedom you have always dreamed of.

Summary

Congratulations on following the process we have outlined in this book! By doing so, you can expect to achieve great success in your property flipping business and grow it to the next level.

- By following the proven strategies, you can minimise risks, maximise profits and establish a successful and sustainable business in the competitive world of property flipping.
- The financial freedom you've always dreamed of is within your reach, and by implementing the

techniques outlined in this book, you can turn your dreams into reality.

- Keep up the good work, and watch your property flipping business soar to new heights!

Conclusion

Throughout this book, I have emphasised the immense benefits of due diligence, finding your ceiling price, sticking to your budget, renovating sustainably and staging your property when flipping it for sale. By incorporating these key practices into your property flipping strategy, you significantly increase the likelihood of a successful and profitable outcome.

With thorough background work, you gain a comprehensive understanding of the property, its potential risks and the market conditions. This knowledge equips you with the information needed to make informed decisions and avoid costly mistakes. By conducting inspections, researching permits and evaluating the neighbourhood and comparable sales, you position yourself for success in the competitive real estate market.

Finding your ceiling price is essential in ensuring a profitable resale. By carefully analysing market trends, assessing property conditions and considering comparable sales, you can determine the maximum amount you should pay for the property. This disciplined approach protects your investment and allows for a comfortable margin to cover renovation costs while maximising potential profits.

Sticking to your budget is crucial for financial discipline and overall project success. Creating a realistic budget and diligently managing expenses throughout the renovation process helps you stay on track and avoid overspending. By allocating funds strategically and prioritising improvements that yield the highest return on investment, you maximise your chances of achieving a favourable financial outcome.

Additionally, staging your property has proven to be such a powerful tool for maximising kerb appeal and optimising your return on investment. By showcasing the property in its best light, creating an inviting and appealing atmosphere, and allowing potential buyers to envision themselves living there, you significantly increase the property's desirability. This has led to quicker sales and almost guaranteed higher offers whenever we have staged properties for developers, which ultimately maximises your financial returns if you do so too.

Time and time again, these practices have proven to be instrumental in achieving success in the property market. By incorporating the heavy lifting before you even purchase your property, and investing in professional staging, you position your property to be sold quickly for the highest possible value.

As you embark on your own property flipping journey, I encourage you to embrace the principles outlined in this book. By making informed decisions before you begin, adhering to your budget and leveraging the power of staging, you set yourself up for success. May the knowledge gained from this book serve as a guide on your path to profitable property flipping ventures, ensuring your properties are sold quickly for the highest possible ROI.

I wish you the utmost success in your new property flipping business, armed with the knowledge and insights gained from this book. May your endeavours be filled with profitable opportunities, wise decisions and rewarding outcomes. Here's to your prosperous journey in the world of property flipping!

ARE YOU READY TO FLIP?

If you are ready to get the maximum profit on your property flip and gain clarity and confidence on its pre-market presentation, why not discover your investor readiness score? It's free and it only takes two minutes.

In return, you will get a free discovery call with our award-winning pre-property listing expert to give you custom-made guidance based on your score. Learn how to avoid the biggest mistakes that are costing your property flipping business time and money, custom made for you.

How it works

- **Answer fifteen questions:** Nice and simple, these questions help us to identify your key strengths and weaknesses for more accurate results.
- **Receive your results:** Once you have finished, your answers are pumped through our clever algorithm to produce your final score.
- **Action steps:** Based on your score, we will provide some insights for you to take action and improve your score for next time.

What we will cover

How strong your pre-listing presentation currently is and how you can improve your score. During our call we will dive deep on all aspects of your property presentation and how you can improve this to get maximum ROI and get your property sold quicker and for more money.

CONCLUSION

During this process, we will take you through our property staging strategy and how you can easily implement it to elevate your asset before putting it on the market ready for viewers.

www.aapropertystage.co.uk

'How to' staging surgery

We also have a 'how to' staging surgery which includes simple videos on how to gain valuable quick wins in key elements of property flipping. These are filled with insider knowledge gained from my many years of experience working in the industry.

To view these, take a look on our social media pages. You never know what you might learn.

Acknowledgements

My husband, Rob: Property developer, proof checker and a calming influence on my hectic mind.

Geraldine Brennan: For patiently and systematically sorting out my jumbled-up words and ideas.

My publisher, Rethink Press: The dream team who quite literally turned my 'dream' of writing a book into a reality.

Daniel Priestley: For teaching me everything I know about how to run a successful business.

Samantha Williamson, Roma Finance: For providing valuable information and always being my loyal fan in promoting the value of my work to others.

Oliver Kersh: For adding the 'golden glow' to my work through his expert photography.

Henry Davis: For all his invaluable knowledge and support on all things auction housing and QS'ing.

Dave Drimmie: My ever-enthusiastic, motivational friend and #GSD buddy.

My sister, Rhonda: For always questioning my ideas and making me think just that little bit harder.

Mark Southgate, MOBIE: For his constant enthusiasm and all the great work he does for MOBIE.

Andy Ardron: For his invaluable feedback and on all things property.

My running friend, Sarah Cassie: For consistently giving me valued feedback on ideas I had while out on long runs in the hills.

My two boys, Hugo and Rowan: Both of you are my sources of motivation. Thank you for keeping me grounded.

The author

Angela Drakeford started her career in interior design after graduating from Leeds Metropolitan University with a degree in interior architecture in 1996. From there, she moved out to Dubai and worked at two of the top-ranked interior design studios in the world. Her work included many of the five-star hotels that are still there today. It was there that she learned that attention to detail was paramount in creating spaces elevated above the ordinary.

When she returned to the UK in 2008, she set up her own design studio and her award-winning property staging business A+A Property Stagers, helping countless developers and homeowners present their properties to maximise their returns. Her emphasis on sustainable renovation and business accruement has evolved over time and is of paramount importance in her business ethos today.

She actively supports the charity MOBIE and in June 2023 ran the Montane Summer Spine Race in 155 hours – an unsupported 270-mile ultra race, the full length of the Pennine Way – to raise money in support of the great work they do.

She regularly gives talks and coaching sessions on how best to present your property post-sale. She also hosts her own staging surgery on Instagram, giving helpful hints and tips on all things relating to property staging.

If you've recently flipped your property and would like to discuss how to present it to gain maximum ROI, get in touch at hello@aapropertystage.co.uk.

- www.aapropertystage.co.uk.
- https://instagram.com/a.a.property.stage
- https://facebook.com/AA.property.stage
- https://linkedin.com/in/angela-drakeford1974/
- https://twitter.com/stagers_a